Bloom of the Diamond Stone

First published 1979 by Pluto Press Limited
Unit 10 Spencer Court, 7 Chalcot Road, London NW1 8LH

Pluto Press gratefully acknowledges financial
assistance from the Calouste Gulbenkian Foundation,
Lisbon, with the publication of this series

ISBN 0 86104 207 7

Designed by Tom Sullivan
Cover designed by Kate Hepburn
Cover picture: 'A girl member of the IRA holding a
flag during yesterday's march to Milltown Cemetery,
Belfast. Her mother is also holding the flag.' *The
Times*, 3 April, 1972 – 'A photograph which directly provoked me to
write a play on the "troubles".'
Wilson John Haire

Printed in Great Britain by Latimer Trend & Company Ltd Plymouth

Wilson John Haire

Bloom of
the Diamond Stone

Pluto  Plays

For Veronica Duffy

A NOTE ON THE AUTHOR

Wilson John Haire was born in Belfast in 1932 in the Protestant ghetto of 'The Hammer' of a Protestant father and a Catholic mother. He entered the Belfast shipyards at the age of fourteen and subsequently served an apprenticeship as a woodworker. He arrived in London in 1954, worked in the construction industry and spent his spare time as an actor and stagehand at Unity Theatre. His plays include *The Clockin' Hen* (Hampstead Theatre, 1968), *The Diamond, Bone and Hammer and Along the Shoughs of Ulster* (Hampstead Theatre, 1968), *Within Two Shadows* (Royal Court, 1972), *Echoes from a Concrete Canyon* (Royal Court, 1975), *Letter from a Soldier* (BBC TV, 1975 and the Orange Tree, Richmond, 1977), *The Dandelion Clock* (BBC TV, 1975) and *Lost Worlds* (Cottesloe Theatre at the National Theatre, 1978). Wilson John Haire won the George Devine Award in 1972 and the *Evening Standard*'s Most Promising Playwright Award in 1973. He was Resident Dramatist at the Royal Court Theatre in 1974.

Bloom of the Diamond Stone

The play begins with two short mummer plays. In *Blind Dawn* the history of nationalist Ireland should be more readily understood because it takes us chronologically through the Great Revolts against the early Danish rule and later English rule. Provo insurrection in Ulster today draws its main inspiration from these centuries. The defeat of the Danes was brought about by the high king Brian Boru who, for the first time, managed to unify his inter-warring chieftains and their numerous principalities into one force for the final onslaught against the enemy. Ireland was united briefly in the twelfth century as it never was before and never has been since. It is reckoned that less violence was required by Fidel Castro to overthrow the criminal regime of Batista than that used by the Provos in Ulster over the past decade. Indeed, many colonial situations throughout the world have disappeared with less effort. Why is this?

In the second mummer play, *Billy's Bike Ride*, you may get a clue to this state of affairs. Protestant history in Ireland goes no further back than the seventeenth century. The Catholic nationalist heroes of ancient history are meaningless to the Protestant. Their hero is King William the Third, of the Dutch House of Orange. William led his early bourgeois forces to Ireland to fight James the Second and his feudalistic forces. Ireland was the chosen cock-pit of Europe for this struggle. Protestantism then, as in the rest of Europe, was enlightenment and the harbinger of coming industrialisation. Industry in Ulster was a native growth from this ideological stance of the New Order. The Protestant tiller of the land started to do a little linen weaving to supplement his income. Eventually the more adventurous forsook the land and set up full time. In the market place the more competitive ate the less able, and then went on to employ them in small groups until, over the years, expansion led to the spinning-mill. Feudal Ireland stuck to the land. The divisions, by the eighteenth century, were concrete. The hands of the clock couldn't be turned back for unity's sake in much the same way that the West's patch-up of feudalism in South-East Asia couldn't hold back the various forms of in-digenous socialism. If England had not become bourgeois when it did, but Ireland had, Irish troops could possibly be patrolling the streets of London with Wembley Stadium being used as an internment camp.

Time, of course, has caught up with events in Ireland. Southern Ireland is no longer feudal, but very much bourgeois; though extremely conservative, it is advancing industrially. The Ulster Protestant is no longer in the vanguard of European liberty with his once joyous demonstrations to celebrate, in the centre of Belfast, the Fall of the Bastille or his rapturous welcome to the emer-gence of the young American Republic. Today he seems strangely disorien-tated as far as mainstream European politics are concerned. Protestant society is now tight-lipped. Its creative artists reveal very little. Popular mar-ket considerations veer some of them towards the Catholic nationalist viewpoint when writing about Ulster. Thus Protestant history is kept submerged leaving the now sectarian slogans on the gable-ends to reveal the tip of the iceberg.

The main play concerns the individual undergoing the sectarian divisions that exist between a group of workers in a Belfast factory. Rosaleen, the mute, oppressed Catholic girl, suffers her own history as well as the history of Jim the Protestant boy. Both, in the long run, amputate themselves from their respective communities through circumstances not of their own making and find there is no neutral ground where enlightenment may live. Two national aspirations cannot be integrated, only mutually recognised. But, by taking nationalism out of the front-line war, a step is made towards realising the true aspirations of class awareness.

Wilson John Haire

The Mummer Plays

These two mummer plays can be played before the opening of the main plays. Alternatively, they can be played in the theatre foyer or in the street in front of the theatre. The characters are played by the characters of *Bloom of the Diamond Stone* (opposite).

Blind Dawn

The Virgin	Rosaleen McGurk
Revivalist Doctor	Sadie Quinn
Philosopher	Matilda McGurk
Fool	The Buck Lep
The Shan Van Vocht	Nuala Quigley
Foiledagainagin	Liam Quinn
A Presenter	
Miniman	A Ventriloquist's Dummy

Billy's Bike Ride

The Spirit of Nineteen Twelve	Jim Sloane
The Late Lord Brookeborough	Helen Shaw
Puffin' Billy	Soldier
A Presenter	

Bloom of the Diamond Stone was first produced at the Abbey Theatre, Dublin, for the Dublin Theatre Festival on 9 October 1973. The cast was as follows:

Rosaleen McGurk	Veronica Duffy
Jim Sloane	Bosco Hogan
Sadie Quinn	Maureen Toal
Matilda McGurk	May Cluskey
The Buck Lep	Philip O'Flynn
Nuala Quigley	Sheelagh Cullen
Helen Shaw	Maire O'Neill
Liam Quinn	Rory Bailey
Soldier	Clive Garaghy
Presenter	Philip O'Sullivan

Directed by Vincent Dowling
Designed by David Wilson

Before The Mummer Plays Begin

The entire cast appear banging drums, blowing bugles and beating tambourines. A Union Jack and Irish Tricolour are carried. Some carry picket boards reading:
TOUTS BEWARE, NO SURRENDER, ULSTER IS BRITISH, MARY, QUEEN OF HEAVEN PRAY FOR US, ALL POWER TO THE PROVOS.

The cast divide into two groups each holding their respective flags. They confront each other.

The group led by the Union Jack sing:

> It is old but it is beautiful, its colours they are fine,
> It was worn at Derry, Aughrim, Enniskillen, and the Boyne,
> My father wore it when a youth in bygone days, of yore,
> So on the twelfth I proudly wear the sash my, my father wore.

The group led by the Irish Tricolour sing:

> Craigavon sent the Specials
> For to shoot the people down
> He thought the IRA were dead
> In dear old Belfast town
> But he had a rude awakening
> With rifle and grenade
> When he met the First Battalion
> Of the Belfast Brigade.

They stand jeering one another and shaking their fists.

A chapel bell tolls. A bass drum is banged six times.

The Mummer Play: Blind Dawn

Presenter

Be calm, be calm!
Youse soon will l'arn
We are the Mummer's Troupe.
Isn't this a lovely barn
For performing our plays
Without the stoop.

On this Feast of the Assumption Day
In the city of Belfast
The politicos lurch on feet of clay
Slabberin', as they glorify the Past.

So, all aboard oul' History's ferry
And we'll start our journey
WITH ... THE ... VIRGIN MARY!

ROSALEEN, *heavily veiled and dressed in a long, blue robe, enters through the screens, carrying a lighted candelabrum, puts it on a table and sits in the armchair.*

MATILDA *enters wearing a dunce's cap and carrying a well-worn, bound volume.*

Philosopher I am the Philosopher. I see all, but all must happen first. The spirit of Man is my concern. (*Circling.*) Mildewed souls as new! Mildewed souls as new!

SADIE *enters wearing a black castor-hat and carrying a doctor's bag.*

Revivalist Doctor I am the Revivalist Doctor. I can plough and dose the dried fields of your flesh. (*Circling and calling out.*) The dead brought back to life! The dead brought back to life!

THE BUCK LEP, *wearing a fool's cap with bells, enters cautiously before leaping into the air and shaking his head.*

Fool I am the Fool of History. No man sees me as I am. (*Crouching.*) First, I am three feet tall. (*Walking on tiptoes.*) Then six feet six. (*Stretching his arms above his head.*) Ten feet. (*Leaping into the air.*) Fifteen feet! (*Lying flat on the ground.*) But ... when I lie I am twelve inches high.

MATILDA *and* SADIE *circle, calling out their wares. They go to the* VIRGIN MARY, *bow, kneel and cross themselves.*

LIAM *enters riding a hobby horse, and wearing a straw mask and shroud. He hangs from the saddle as if wounded.*

NUALA *with a hump and wearing a long, black cloak with cowl, supports him.*

The Shan Van Vocht I am THE SHAN VAN VOCHT . . . Ireland is also my name.

Foiledagainagin I am Foiledagainagin. I was born yesterday, and today . . . and I shall be born again tomorrow – for I am many men. Right now, I am Brian Boru. A few minutes ago, in the year Ten-fourteen, a treacherous Dane drove a bronze sword between my ribs. (*Clutching the shoulder of* THE SHAN VAN VOCHT.) We were to marry.

The Shan Van Vocht (*calling out*) Save my hero!

The hobby horse rears at the sight of the prostrate FOOL, *throwing* FOILEDAGAINAGIN *to the ground with a groan.*

Rise, Fool, and bring me your quack.

THE REVIVALIST DOCTOR *rushes in and mistakenly goes to the* FOOL, *opens her bag and takes out a saw. He promptly jumps to his feet.*

Revivalist Doctor Another miracle cure!

The Shan Van Vocht (*calling out as she shakes* FOILEDAGAINAGIN) Save my lover, doctor!

THE REVIVALIST DOCTOR *rushes over and sits beside him. She holds the saw as she feels for a part to cut and reacts as if nothing is below the shroud. She takes out a bottle of medicine and tries to pour it down his throat, but it only runs on to the ground.*

Revivalist Doctor No place to make an incision nor make a river of his throat. Go quick and bring his body before he is out of this world.

The Shan Van Vocht (*calling out*) Somebody help!

Philosopher (*approaching and looking down at* FOILEDAGAINAGIN) This ghost drips of white blood . . . Like the droppings of a blackbird on a winter tree.

The FOOL *lets out a loud laugh, bends his knees and runs around in circles.*

Revivalist Doctor Nothing but the wind will whistle under this winding sheet now.

Fool (*jeering*) You have used up the eleventh century.

The Shan Van Vocht (*crying*) Bring my hero back.

Philosopher (*looking through her book*) Twelve-fifteen, Thirteen-eighteen – No good. Wait! (*Shutting the book.*) Brian Boru, you are no more. Rise once more and fight the Saxon!

Foiledagainagin (*rising and yawning*) One more war and we are free. (*He mounts the hobby horse and rides in circles.*)

The FOOL *collapses laughing.*

The Shan Van Vocht (*running after* FOILEDAGAINAGIN) Stop! Wait for me! (*Stopping in front of the* PHILOSOPHER.) Who is he now?

The bass drum beats.

Philosopher Robert Emmett.

The Shan Van Vocht Thank you . . . Oh, thank you!

Philosopher Hurry! You might catch him before Eighteen-oh-three.

The Shan Van Vocht (*running after him*) Marriage before martyrdom!

Revivalist Doctor Trade is bad – they leave their bodies on the battlefield. Yesterday . . . always yesterday.

Philosopher Yesterday is the graveyard of the body but today is the nursery of the soul.

The FOOL *shrieks with laughter.*

Revivalist Doctor (*to* FOOL) I'll catch you yet.

Fool (*dancing around*) You'll run out of history. You wait and see. (*He leaps across the floor, laughing.*)

Philosopher (*calling out*) Mildewed souls as new, mildewed souls as new!

Revivalist Doctor Dead brought back to life, dead brought back to life!

FOILEDAGAINAGIN *approaches, on his hobby horse, bent and feeble and supported by* THE SHAN VAN VOCHT.

The Shan Van Vocht Too late! Too late!

Fool Another re-tread?

The FOOL *throws up his arms, making the horse shy, and throwing* FOILEDAGAINAGIN *to the ground.*

The Shan Van Vocht (*shrieking*) HELP!

Revivalist Doctor (*appearing with a huge bottle of medicine*) A new miracle drug. Good for backache, bonebreak, rancid liver, St Vitus Dance, club feet, impotence, incompetence, incontinence, short legs, loose tongues, lost causes, loose limbs –

She attempts to pour it down FOILEDAGAINAGIN's *throat but it runs on to the ground. She rises disgusted.*

Not another empty sheet! Without even the husk of a louse under it.

Philosopher (*entering and opening her book*) Hurry, it's one minute to Nineteen-sixteen. Robert Emmett no more. Once more rise . . . PADRAIC PEARSE!

FOILEDAGAINAGIN *slowly rises yawning and mounts his horse clumsily.*

Foiledagainagin (*whirling his sword around his head*) 'The fools, the fools, they have left us our Fenian dead, and while Ireland holds these graves, Ireland unfree shall never be at peace!'

He rides in circles.

The Shan Van Vocht (*running after him*) Have the Banns been read? Did you buy the ring?

The FOOL *runs after her, grabbing her by the hips and making her shriek.*

Foiledagainagin (*reining up his horse*) Beware, Fool, or I'll deal you a death blow.

The FOOL *promptly collapses on the ground and feigns death.*

FOILEDAGAINAGIN *rides off.*

THE SHAN VAN VOCHT *starts to follow but stops and goes back and bends over the* FOOL.

He suddenly grabs her, pulls her down and mounts her.

Fool Now I take a journey that will add a new dimension to that creature known as Man. I shall shunt this nation to quieter waters.

1st Voice Dirty oul' brute!

2nd Voice Leave that wee woman alone!

3rd Voice Like dogs in the street.

1st Voice It's a bloody disgrace!

The FOOL *helps* THE SHAN VAN VOCHT *to her feet. They both walk around arms entwined around one another.*

Foiledagainagin (*approaching, hanging from his horse*) I am going! (*Falling on the ground.*) With acknowledgements to a British firing squad.

Philosopher (*passing*) Mildewed souls as new!

Revivalist Doctor (*passing*) Dead brought back to life!

Foiledagainagin (*crying out feebly*) Water, water.

Revivalist Doctor 'Tis only a sheet again. (*Pulling at it.*) You should keep it more clean though . . . wherever you exist.

Philosopher (*looking down at him*) I can do nothing more for him. The old model isn't made anymore. Why don't you tidy yourself up! (*To the* REVIVALIST DOCTOR.) Help me to the launderette with him. (*They pull him up, help him on his horse, support him on either side and walk away.*) Hurry before the Historians come.

The Shan Van Vocht (*approaching and holding her stomach*) Where's the mid-wife! (*She circles before collapsing.*) Oh . . . hurry!

Revivalist Doctor (*running to her and massaging her stomach*) Are the pains getting closer, daughter?

Philosopher Look! The water is breaking.

THE SHAN VAN VOCHT *lets out a wild screech. The* REVIVALIST DOCTOR *pulls a ventriloquist's doll from under the clothes of* THE SHAN VAN VOCHT, *holds it upside down and slaps it on the back.*

Miniman (*singing*) 'Rise up, rise up, for I've come to lead youse. For Ireland's freedom we live or die.'

Philosopher (*surprised*) AGAIN!

Miniman But first we have a drink.

Revivalist Doctor A bottle of stout?

Miniman To hell with your peasant's piss! I suggest a good French wine . . . and an old year to boot.

The Shan Van Vocht (*taking the ventriloquist's dummy and cuddling it*) My baby is speaking already!

Miniman Hello there, Mother, nice to see you.

The Shan Van Vocht Coup, coup, coup, who's Mammy's wee man.

She takes out her breast to feed him.

Miniman A thousand scunders on your breast! Take me to your best restaurant.

Revivalist Doctor 'The Pepper Mill'?

Miniman A hangout for the petit-bourgeoisie! Let's have a banquet at the Europa Hotel.

The Shan Van Vocht I can't afford to feed him. What will I do?

Revivalist Doctor (*taking the saw out of her bag*) Cut his tongue out.

The Shan Van Vocht (*clasping* MINIMAN *tightly to her breast*) No . . . my baby!

Philosopher I have a better idea. Let's take him to the Virgin Mary. She'll look after him . . . that'll change his outlook. (*They approach the* VIRGIN *cautiously.*) Hail, Holy Queen, Mother of Mercy, Assumed Body and Soul into Heaven! We honour you on this, Your Feast of the Assumption Day.

Revivalist Doctor O, Most Gracious Virgin, listen to our pleas!

Philosopher Lady of Lourdes –

Revivalist Doctor Our Lady of Fatima –

Philosopher Take this child as your own.

They kneel and pray before her.

The VIRGIN *takes the child in her arms. They arise, bend one knee before her, cross themselves and back slowly away from her.*

Miniman Mother, where do babies come from – ? (*The voice trails off into baby gurgles.*)

Blackout.

Lights up. The VIRGIN *wears a large cloak.*

Presenter

> Let's present a lovely lad
> With his nationalist education
> Sixteen years old –
> Ach, he can't be bad
> despite being five times on probation.

The VIRGIN *opens her cloak to reveal* FOILEDAGAINAGIN *sitting on her knee.*

He wears a dark-blue anorak and a black hood over his head. Two bandoliers of ammunition criss-cross his chest.

He mounts his hobby horse. The VIRGIN *kisses him on the cheek and wipes away the tears below her veil.*

Foiledagainagin (*waving to her as she rides off*) Goodbye, Mother. (*He rides away as if on a long journey.*)

The FOOL, *a sword in his belt, walks by, reading a horse-racing newspaper.*

Hey, oul' hand! Is this the right way for the Falls Road?

Fool You're in it, fella.

Foiledagainagin Does a man wearing a fool's cap live anywhere around here?

Fool (*thinking*) A man wearing a fool's cap –? (*Dropping his paper.*) Christ, that's me!

He starts to run. FOILEDAGAINAGIN *rides after him.*

(*Stopping to beat the ground with his fists.*) Let me in! Let me in!

Foiledagainagin There's only Hell down there. (*Drawing his gun.*) Let me open a door for you.

Revivalist Doctor (*rushing in between them*) Don't you recognise your own midwife!

Foiledagainagin I am on my way to the Front but first I must settle accounts with the rapist of my mother.

Philosopher Mildewed souls as new –!

Foiledagainagin (*trying to get at the* FOOL) At last I'm on the muddy path to history!

Philosopher (*rushing over*) Let's talk of the Mysteries of Being –

Foiledagainagin Go ahead.

Philosopher The Riddle of the Universe is – The Meaning of Life – We are here because – because –

Foiledagainagin Go on.

Philosopher There's a lot of power in prayer.

Foiledagainagin Impotent like the rest!

The Shan Van Vocht (*rushing over*) Who is this young man?

Foiledagainagin I have come to deal a mortal blow to the Saxon and all his underlings.

The Shan Van Vocht My hero!

Foiledagainagin A moment.

He rushes at the FOOL. *The* FOOL *draws his sword and swipes at him.* FOILEDAGAINAGIN *dodges whilst trying to draw a bead on him.*

Philosopher Boy, you're fighting your own father.

The Shan Van Vocht Go on, don't heed her.

Revivalist Doctor Your mother eggs you on!

Foiledagainagin (*firing*) Oedipus . . . my high hole!

The FOOL *falls.* FOILEDAGAINAGIN *mounts his horse and* THE SHAN VAN VOCHT *climbs on behind him.*

They ride around.

The Shan Van Vocht Does it seem to be getting dark to you? Ride on, ride on!
Foiledagainagin My eyes, my eyes!
The Shan Van Vocht It's only a total eclipse of the sun. Ride on!

They continue to ride in great swerving circles.

The PHILOSOPHER *and the* REVIVALIST DOCTOR *throw stones at them before the horse disappears.*

The VIRGIN *breaks down weeping.*

Fool Their horizon is as high as I am now.

His body jerks and he is still.

Revivalist Doctor (*rushing over to him*) Get up, you eejit you! You've just been elected to parliament.

The FOOL *springs to his feet.*

A bass drum beats six times.

Over immediately to **Billy's Bike Ride.**

The Mummer Play: Billy's Bike Ride

Two hitch-hikers stand on a country road.

JIM SLOANE *wears his usual denims but with a bowler hat on his head and an Orange Sash around his neck. He holds up a large cut-out of the Red Hand of Ulster, with the thumb in the hitch-hiking position.*

HELEN SHAW *is dressed as a starchy matron of the Northern Protestant middle-classes.*

They stand some distance from one another.

Presenter
>By a country road
>Stands Ulster's true-blue son
>He works in a factory just for fun.
>Nearby stands a Loyalist matron
>With wheens of stocks and shares
>In caterin'.

The noise of a heavy lorry passing.

The Spirit of Nineteen Twelve Stop, Lord Jesus, stop! Don't you know I'm the Spirit of Nineteen Twelve?

THE LATE LORD BROOKEBOROUGH *haughtily watches the lorry pass.*

(*Going to her.*) You'll never get a lift like that, misses.

The Late Lord Brookeborough I'm not used to being addressed like that . . . I'm the Late Lord Brookeborough.

The Spirit of Nineteen Twelve I'm tellin' you, Misses, that's the fourteenth lorry that's passed this hour.

The Late Lord Brookeborough Do you mind moving away. Who's going to pick me up with the likes of you about.

The Spirit of Nineteen Twelve (*looking closely at her*) Protestant or teague?

The Late Lord Brookeborough How dare you . . . unsubtle hooligan.

The Spirit of Nineteen Twelve I bloody well asked you a question!

FOILEDAGAINAGIN *and* THE SHAN VAN VOCHT *approach on the hobby horse.*

THE SPIRIT OF NINETEEN TWELVE *sticks out his 'Red Hand' sign but soon abandons the idea when he recognises them. Shouting after them:*

If I ever see youse again it will be too soon!

The Late Lord Brookeborough (*watching them go*) Unsoapables! Lazy good-for-nothings. Breeding like sex maniacs . . . with every birth a shipwreck!

(*As* THE SPIRIT OF NINETEEN TWELVE *approaches.*) Don't you come near me!

The Spirit of Nineteen Twelve Couldn't help hearin' what you were sayin' about them 'uns. Ay, you're right there, Misses. Thought you looked like one of us.

The Late Lord Brookeborough (*waving her hand*) Just move away.

Presenter
>They want a lift to Sixteen-ninety
>When things seemed very elementary
>But the roads round here are very hilly –
>Look out, lads!
>There's PUFFIN' BILLY!

A drum beats frantically.

The SOLDIER *appears dressed as King William the Third. He rides a bicycle and is breathing heavily.*

He stops and gets off painfully as THE SPIRIT OF NINETEEN TWELVE *sticks out the 'Red Hand'.*

The Spirit of Nineteen Twelve Oul' hand – I mean Your Majesty – give us a lift on the bar of your bike.

Puffin' Billy (*gasping for air before speaking in a heavy Dutch accent*)
>I, King Villiam the Third, Prince of Orange,
>with my forces consisting of native
>Protestants and German Protestant
>mercenaries defeated, most decisively,
>the feudalistic forces of James the
>Second, at the Battle of the Boyne . . .
>in Sixteen-ninety.
>I paved the way for your new Bourgeoisie
>Order. You have done vell . . . but, a few
>seconds ago – How do you say –? Fifty years
>ago.

He takes a pinch of snuff from an ornate snuff box, sniffs it and sneezes into a lace handkerchief.

The Spirit of Nineteen Twelve What are you talkin' about, wee lad –! I mean Your Majesty?

Puffin' Billy (*to himself*) Vhere am I?

The Late Lord Brookeborough Ulster, sire.

Puffin' Billy And the River Boyne?

The Late Lord Brookeborough (*pointing down the road*) They have it.

Puffin' Billy Vell, can you beat that!

The Spirit of Nineteen Twelve What's he talkin' about?

The Late Lord Brookeborough (*clapping her hands in ecstasy*) What a joy to meet an intellectual!

Puffin' Billy Ma . . . dam, I am a tired man. Celestially, I ride the skyways on two vheels without the comfort of my four-footer –

The Late Lord Brookeborough (*thinking*) The Fall of the Bastille –

Puffin' Billy Ja, Ja –

The Late Lord Brookeborough The French followed your example, sire.

Puffin' Billy (*impatiently*) Ja, ja, ja, ja –!

The Late Lord Brookeborough The lights went on all over Europe that day – (*Quickly, in a whisper.*) Give a genteel lady a lift to the next stage of our struggle, sire.

Puffin' Billy Ma . . . dam, you don't seem to understand. I can do no more for you.

The Spirit of Nineteen Twelve Hey there! What are youse talkin' about?

The Late Lord Brookeborough (*indicating* THE SPIRIT OF NINETEEN TWELVE) Poor illiterate boy.

Puffin' Billy (*to himself in despair whilst adjusting his bicycle clips*) How can this be! (*Feeling the tyres of his bicycle.*) Fit your jigsaw piece of Ulster into Europe . . . (*Shouting.*) And let me get to bed!

The Spirit of Nineteen Twelve Give us a ride, mister, before it's too late. (*He tries to get on the bar of the bike.*)

The Late Lord Brookeborough (*struggling with him*) Ladies first!

Puffin' Billy Gott in Himmel! And me with a flat tyre, too.

All three fall over the bicycle.

Puffin' Billy rises first, runs with the bicycle, throws his leg over it, and rides off.

The Spirit of Nineteen Twelve (*shouting after him*) I don't understand what you mean, but for Christ's sake give us a slogan before you go!

The Late Lord Brookeborough Stupid! Stupid! You made me so ashamed in front of the gentleman with your idiot talk . . . and he was ready to give me a lift. (*In anguish.*) What will I do now?

The Spirit of Nineteen Twelve (*going towards her in a menacing way*) Arse lickers! While youse were having tea on the lawns of Stormont, we were livin' like pigs in shite –

The Late Lord Brookeborough (*putting her hands over her ears*) The language, the language!

The Spirit of Nineteen Twelve You taught us nothing about the history of our Protestant people. (*Cynically.*) The coalfields of England, the Thames rises in the upper reaches of . . . the upper reaches of – Arse lickers! We had to learn our history in the streets. (*Rapidly.*) Fuck the Pope, fuck the Pope, FUCK THE POPE, FUCK THE POPE, FUCK THE POPE –

THE LATE LORD BROOKEBOROUGH *runs off screaming.*

The entire cast of both Mummer plays gather to sing the chorus as he starts singing to the tune of 'I Was Born Under a Wandering Star'.

I was born under the Union Jack.

Cast   He was born under the Union Jack.

The Spirit of Nineteen Twelve

Do you know where Hell is?

Hell is up the Falls

Kill all the popeheads

And we'll guard oul' Derry's walls.

Cast   He was born under the Union Jack

The Union, Union Jack.

The Spirit of Nineteen Twelve

The Falls were made for burnin'

The Teagues are there to kill.

Cast (*shouting it out*)

Is there a better road –!

The Spirit of Nineteen Twelve

– Like the Shankill.

I was born under the Union Jack.

Cast   He was born under the Union Jack.

The Spirit of Nineteen Twelve

If guns are made for shootin'

Then skulls are made to crack

You'll never see a better Teague

Than, with a bullet in his back.

I was born under the Union Jack.

Cast   The Union, Union Jack.

A lorry approaches. He sticks out the 'Red Hand' but the lorry passes on.

The Spirit of Nineteen Twelve Dutch licence plates? What the HELL is going on?

The cast, one by one, hold up large placards reading E.U.R.O.P.E.

Cast (*shouting*) EUROPE!

Blackout.

Bloom of the Diamond Stone

ACT I

SCENE 1

A pop song plays over the sound of factory machinery. The curtain opens.

In the corner of the factory at a work-bench, ROSALEEN MCGURK, *a dark-haired girl with burning eyes, aged nineteen, works a hand-operated machine for riveting pieces of metal used in delicate electronic equipment.*

Also nick-named 'The Stone' because of her silent and uncommunicative ways, she stands feeding the machine and throwing the finished article into metal crates on the bench.

The music plays on, relayed, from a radio programme.

ROSALEEN *suddenly clutches her finger and uncovers it slowly, almost afraid to look at the blood.*

She hides her hand as NUALA QUIGLEY, *a joyful girl of her own age, approaches singing in time to the music.*

Nuala God, that's lovely. (*Louder.*) Lovely! (*She entwines her arms around herself and slowly revolves her body in time to the music. Catching sight of her.*) Rosaleen! You've cut yourself. (*Still swaying she grasps her finger and examines it.*)

HELEN SHAW, *the supervisor, a woman of thirty, approaches.*

Helen Nuala Quigley, what are you doing up here!

Nuala Rosaleen here has near cut the hand off herself, Miss Shaw.

Helen So you heard the blood drip from the Soldering Room? Go and get the first-aid box.

NUALA *goes.*

Let's see your hand. Worse has been seen. It should mend before the day is out.

NUALA *returns with the box.*

(*To* NUALA.) Put a plaster on it and listen to no dying speeches . . . and don't let me find you up here again, Quigley.

NUALA *sticks her tongue out behind her back as she goes.*

Nuala (*fixing her finger*) Couldn't you have screeched, raised the hair on their heads, wept buckets, girned . . . just one wee tear, one totey wee tear – Oh, they are right here! You are a 'stone'. A safe without a key. But I'll look after you – Not just because I promised your mother. We teagues must stick together – The supervisor's lookin' down. Will you be all right? Oh, that bitch! She's starin' daggers at me silent.

She moves off swaying to the music.

JIM SLOANE, *age twenty, wearing blue denim trousers, a denim jacket, with an open-necked shirt and heavy boots, approaches, pulling a trolley loaded with metal crates.*

He nears the bench and looks up and down the factory warily.

Jim Get them relays finished, you fenian bitch you.

ROSALEEN *looks at him impassionately a moment before turning to her work.*

(*Looking cautiously around before whispering.*) See this. (*He pulls the chain, around his neck, from under his shirt, and shows her the live bullet at the end of it.*) Point three O three! Live! I promised this to the first teague found up the Shankill. This is my chain of office. I'm the leader of the Shower of Hail gang. See it? Look at it –!

Nuala (*approaching silently*) Put it away, Jim Sloane, or it'll be in you . . . not on you. (*Patting his face gently.*) I know who you are.

Jim (*stepping back*) Would that be a threat?

Nuala Could be.

Jim (*uncertain, he looks at her a moment before lunging forward and trying to put his hand up her dress*) Give us a feel . . . a good grope. Go on.

She shrieks and breaks away. He runs after her.

(*Coming back and lifting a crate off the bench.*) She's near one of us . . . I swear it. (*Going close to her.*) Youse Catholic girls – (*He puts out his hand to touch her.* ROSALEEN *takes his hand and shakes it. Bewildered.*) What's goin' on! Are you on your 'geg' or something.

Helen (*approaching*) Get that lot into the Inspection Room, Sloane.

Jim (*shouting*) I've got a bloody handle to my jug!

He quickly loads the crates and departs.

Helen (*taken back*) What! (*Following him.*) Commere you here – Cheeky Shankill Road slum-dweller. You won't speak to me like that.

ROSALEEN *works the machine.*

(*Coming back.*) Did he come back this way? Who does he think he is! I'm in charge here. (*Wiping a hand over her eyes.*) I'll tell my boyfriend on him.

ROSALEEN *looks silently at her.*

All right, get on with your work. (*She goes.*)

ROSALEEN *looks at her watch and switches off the machine. The sounds of the factory machines start to die away, one by one. The music goes off. The silence is shattered by the lunch-time electric klaxon.*

NUALA *appears carrying two cups of tea and a pack of sandwiches.*

ROSALEEN *sits on the bench unwrapping her sandwiches.* NUALA *sits beside her.*

Nuala Finger all right? Did you see the new electrician this mornin'. He's a lovely fella. I don't know what he is but I'm sure he's one of 'them' . . . doesn't alter the fact that he's lovely. (*Whispering.*) I think Lizzie's pregnant . . . caught her lookin' at her belly in the toilet mirror. She's pale lookin' this last two mornin's, and, I'll swear I saw her cleanin' up the spew in the Testin' Room. God, I can't wait till I find out who put her on the benefit books! And do you know what else –?

JIM *arrives, carefully pulling his empty trolley on which he has balanced his cup of tea.*

He sits on the trolley a number of yards from them and opens his lunch tin. What does 'he' want! Don't look at him. (*Loudly to* ROSALEEN.) Nice day isn't it . . . and it'll be dark again tonight. (*She pretends to whisper.*)

JIM *sits staring at them a while. He breaks off a piece of bread and throws it, hitting* ROSALEEN. NUALA *continues whispering. He throws another piece of bread.*

Leave her alone, you! (*She continues whispering.*)

He hits ROSALEEN *with a third piece of bread.*

Why aren't you sittin' with the rest of the Protestants!

Jim (*opening up his sandwich*) Take a dekko at this! Pilchards again . . . soaked into the bread it has. My oul' doll has no sense . . . she makes them at night. It'll be tomatoes tomorrow and then the day after that . . . sandwich spread. It's enough to make you 'boke' up. My da . . . he's a hard man . . . even he won't complain. He did once. She floored him. I nearly laughed my leg off . . . he near beat the shite out of me –

Nuala Have you no manners! We're eatin' now.

Jim Had my coat on headin' for the 'Royal' . . . thought I'd busted a rib. Brother says ah – Says ah . . . try laughin' and if you feel something move, get your skates on and take what's left of you to the bone man. (*He falls silent.*)

Nuala (*who has been pretending to whisper, stops, and looks over at him*) Well!

Jim Well what? (*He moves his trolley nearer to them.*)

Nuala Did something move!

Jim Nah.

NUALA *raises her eyes to the ceiling and inhales deeply.*

It was only the bone in my big toe that was cracked. I was fairly laughin' when my oul' da came back and gave me a shove. That's when I felt the pain. 'You've crippled me for life, Da.' Wish I had a picture of his face now . . . ready to blubber like a wee 'bahby'. Gave me a packet of 'fegs,' promised to get me 'stoscious' and bring me pigeon racin' to Ballynahinch. (*Moving his trolley closer.*) He's not a bad oul' spud.

Nuala Better now?

Jim What?

Nuala Your big toe.

Jim Yes.

Nuala Yes?

Jim Ay. (*He falls silent, puts his arms around his knees and his head in his lap.*)

Nuala (*to* ROSALEEN) Goin' to 'The Searched House' tonight?

Jim Where?

Nuala You wouldn't know about that.

Jim Is it a disco . . . I like discos . . . goin' tonight?

Nuala Not with you.

Jim I wouldn't mind goin' along.

Nuala Couldn't.

Jim Why not?

Nuala You'd be as sure as dead.

Jim Oh – (*He unconsciously twiddles the bullet between his fingers.*)

Nuala That's certain . . . isn't it, Rosaleen?

Jim Why doesn't she ever say anything!

Nuala Mind your own business. (*She starts whispering to* ROSALEEN.)

Jim We've got a great disco in our street. We record direct from the radio because the 'sounds' out of the shop can be a bit behind. The brother picks up America for the latest ones there . . . he searches the waves most nights. We've got our own 'Top Twenty'. (*Moving closer. Excitedly.*) You know, we sometimes get the top record . . . even before the D.J.'s do –

Nuala (*stopping whispering suddenly*) God, I'd like to hear them!

Jim I couldn't take the tape-recorder here . . . brother wouldn't let me.

Nuala I could always slip up to your –

Jim Couldn't.

Nuala Oh.

ROSALEEN *moves her lips excitedly.*

Jim She nearly spoke!

Nuala (*finger to her mouth as she watches her*) Shoo!

They wait in silence.

A loud explosion in the distance.

They jump to their feet and stand statue-still, listening.

Helen (*running in agitated*) Where was that bomb!

Nuala Sounded like a seventy-pounder.

Helen Oh! My sister's working in the city centre . . . my mother's shopping there! (*Almost whispering.*) My brother –

Nuala I don't think it was in the city centre, Miss Shaw.

Helen How do YOU know! (*To* JIM.) What are you doing talking to them.

Jim (*trembling and stuttering*) I'll round up my gang tonight, Helen.

Helen (*near hysteria*) Don't call me Helen –! Oh! It doesn't matter, it doesn't matter, Jim.

She rushes off, her hands on her head.

Jim See what youse have done. (*He angrily pulls his trolley away.*)

Nuala (*shouting after him*) How do you know it was our bomb! (*To* ROSALEEN.) Not my bomb. What are they makin' us say, Rosaleen?

The electric klaxon blares loudly. The girls hug each other in fright. A gentle romantic song plays.

Female Voice (*shrill and hysterical in the depths of the factory*) Put off that music!

The music dies away and there is silence. The only sound is ROSALEEN *trying to re-start her machine.*

SCENE 2

A living-room termed a kitchen, in a 'two up, two down' kitchen-house in a Catholic ghetto. A minimum of furniture, a Sacred Heart lamp, a crucifix, the photograph of a man aged about thirty, draped in black.

MATILDA MCGURK, *a work-worn woman in her mid-forties lies on the floor as a nearby gun-battle continues.*

SADIE QUINN, *in her thirties, bursts into the room, half crouched and throws herself on the floor beside* MATILDA.

Sadie It's Albert Street! (*Pausing for breath.*) I was leggin' it through there, to my sister's, when suddenly it went all quiet – like a Christmas Sunday. Every window had its blind pulled . . . pigeons were mad in the sky . . . dogs were pawin' – in the doors . . . soldiers' faces were turnin' amber – All the signs were there for an ambush.

Matilda It's the high-velocity strays I don't like.

Sadie (*listening*) It's dyin' away.

The beating of dustbin lids and the blowing of whistles is followed by the high-pitched sirens of armoured cars.

Matilda Troops! Are they goin' to start searchin' again?

Sadie I'll bolt the door –

Matilda I never bolt the door, Sadie. (*Listening.*) They've passed the end of the street. (*She rises.*)

Sadie (*rising*) They'll be back.

Matilda No, I never bolt the door. They say it wouldn't be hard to get back from the centre of the city, without touchin' the streets, by way of kitchens and parlours, movin' over a highway of cheap, patterned linoleum and hire-purchase carpet –

Sadie And you could tell which street you were in by the smell of Ardglass herrin's fryin' away in Mrs Dwyer's –

Matilda Ay, sure I know that –

Sadie Or you could always look at the rent book behind the clock on the mantelpiece –

Matilda Ay, surely, and, if you were really stuck you could always ask some oul' lad watchin' television from his armchair –

Sadie I know well –

Matilda So I'm told.

Sadie That's right.

Matilda I suppose, the same as myself, you leave a flask of tea with some sandwiches in case of night travellers –

Sadie It's a desperate important thing to do last thing at night.

Matilda It's a month since mine was touched – I wouldn't be doing it . . . but it's neighbour's kids.

Sadie The less said the better, Matilda.

Two shots sound and LIAM QUINN, *a boy of sixteen, bursts into the kitchen from the street carrying a smoking pistol, and looks wildly around.*

Liam 'Lo, Mrs McGurk – Ach hullo, Mammy.

He dashes through the kitchen and out.

Matilda Jesus Christ save us this day and this night! Your wee Liam as well.

Sadie It seems only yesterday he was an altar-boy servin' Mass –

Matilda And stealin' the altar wine.

Sadie (*averting her eyes*) God, I hope he hasn't done it again!

Matilda (*crossing herself while looking steadily at her*) I hope that's all it is.

Sadie Since his father died he's been a handful.

Matilda (*looking at her questioningly*) Mothers still have some influence in this country.

Sadie God, I was red in the face when the priest came to the door lookin' for him. I thought I'd have to send him to England –

Matilda (*listening to the squeal of brakes outside*) Now England's come to him.

Shouted orders outside and a loud banging on the door before it is pushed open roughly. A SOLDIER, *in his late twenties, his face blacked out, leans against the doorpost clutching a rifle with a telescopic sight.*

An army radio periodically crackles with static and incoherent messages behind him in the street.

Soldier (*resigned*) I know you two ladies ain't seen nothing.

Sadie What would you be lookin' for?

Soldier A bleedin' unicorn.

Matilda I know . . . something like a horse –

Soldier With a great bleedin' horn in the middle of its poxy head – Forget it!

Sadie We can talk no more to you, soldier.

Matilda (*to* SOLDIER) What's –

Sadie (*holding the door open, roughly*) Search or go!

Soldier (*to* MATILDA) Cheers. (*He goes.*)

Matilda God, did he look tired!

Sadie Hmmmmmmph!

Matilda (*looking at the black-draped photograph before turning angrily away*)
Men! Almost fifteen years dead. He'd be well up in years now . . . probably
with a crippled foot on him. Can you imagine being up in the night,
bathein' and pamperin' it, and it beelin' red . . . topped with an oul'
girny face, after a night without sleep, starin' at you across the oceans of
plastic table cloth like a brown-paper moon . . . with so many wrinkles
in his brow he could screw his cap on. Sure, it would take you to be away
in the head to even give it kennel room in the yard.

Sadie God, that's a shame on you, misses.

Matilda Soft you'd have to be, and be paralysed north, east, south and west.

Sadie (*crossing herself*) God have mercy on us!

LIAM *re-enters the kitchen.*

Liam (*chuckling*) They're streets away. I'll wait a minute and then go.

Matilda (*flying at him and slapping him about the head*) What the bloody hell
is goin' on around here!

Liam (*trying to dodge*) Lay off, Mrs McGurk!

Matilda (*slapping him*) I put iodine on your skinned knees that time you were
four years old.

Sadie That's enough, Matilda.

Liam (*moving towards the door*) I'll go into the street.

Sadie (*rushing at him and grabbing him by the ear*) You fuckin' well will not!
(*Pushing him roughly into the centre of the room.*) You have me cursin'
in a shrine to our republican dead. (*She looks to the photo and crosses
herself.*)

Matilda (*quiet and menacing*) You sit down there.

Sadie You do what Mrs McGurk tells you.

Matilda You bad boy, I'll give you a pair of red ears.

Sadie (*pulling him by the hair*) You sit there quiet!

Matilda Who put you on the hobby horses every time that hungry horse
dragged the carousel into this very street.

Sadie See what Mrs McGurk done for you.

Matilda Sixpence wasn't easy to come by in those days.

Sadie Bad boy.

Matilda Look at me when I'm talkin' to you.

Sadie Bad boy!

Matilda Wait till it's safe to go.

Sadie Do you hear what Mrs McGurk is sayin' to you!

Matilda Here . . . have a paris bun . . . you don't deserve it.

ROSALEEN *enters quietly.*

Liam 'Lo, Rosaleen.

Matilda (*to* LIAM) Did you say something!

ROSALEEN *exits to a back room.*

Sadie There's your daughter safe and sound.

Matilda Safe . . . but little sound. (*To* LIAM.) Who told you you could listen in. (*She cautiously peeps into the street.*) You can go now . . . you bad rascal.

Sadie (*combing his hair*) Look at the state of you!

Liam Oooow . . . ooooow!

Sadie (*as he is going*) Don't you touch that cooked ham now, when you get home. That's for your uncle and auntie's visit. (LIAM *goes.* ROSALEEN *peeps into the kitchen before withdrawing. Whispering.*) How long is it now?

Matilda Four years.

Sadie As long as that already! Ach, maybe it was the fright of the comin' troubles.

Matilda It's not as if she was brought up amongst a blinded, soundless people who crocheted by touch.

Sadie Maybe when the war is over –

Matilda And . . . it's not as if she ever saw any of us stand shiverin', like a dog pissin' in the snow, at the sound of gunfire. (*Going to the photo.*) What have you got to say about it, Sean.

Sadie Oh God, be careful, Matilda!

Matilda We'll have to face them some day, Sadie.

Sadie Jesus, that would put the shivers up a body, misses!

Matilda I've lain with you in the grave too long, Sean.

Sadie (*jumping to her feet*) You can't say things like that!

Matilda Oh . . . and why!

Sadie Sean belongs to us all now.

Matilda (*shouting*) Have him then! (*She pulls the photo on to the floor. Frightened,* SADIE *exits quickly.*)

Matilda (*loudly*) Martyrs! If they don't die today, they'll be on the labour exchange tomorrow.

ROSALEEN, *on her knees, carefully lifts the photograph and puts it back on the wall.*

SCENE 3

A Catholic shebeen – a makeshift counter with bottles of spirits, packs of canned beer, wooden tables, forms and chairs. A large reproduction of a photograph shows the silhouette of a sitting man, rifle between his knees, watching a burned building.

A large painted sign names the place as 'The Searched House'. A pop song plays on a record player.

NUALA *sways gently to the music.* LIAM, *acting as barman, watches her.*

THE BUCK LEP, *a man in his early forties, wearing working clothes and a flat cap, sits quietly reading his paper.*

Nuala (*without stopping*) Servin' Ireland tonight again, Liam.

Liam The O/C put me on bar duty. Just like any other bloody army – 'Hands up who can handle their drink.' 'Joe Soap' puts his hand up. 'Bar duty at The Searched House.' Some oul' bastard was banging the door at half past seven this mornin', lookin' for a glass of whiskey. The law's well busted around here. Can you imagine two saracens and a company of Brits comin' here to look for the drink licence!

Nuala Wee man with the big coat.

Liam I've been promised some trainin'. We'll be taken to shoot up the troops at 'Silver City'. (*Chuckling.*) It's like a sieve with the bullet holes in it. It'll be the first time I've been under fire – deliberate fire I mean. Death was only shufflin' the cards then but this time I'll be dealt a hand.

Nuala Will your mammy let you go.

Liam (*coming out from behind the counter*) You'll believe me some day.

Nuala (*mocking*) Your shirt-tail is hangin' out.

He hastily feels for it but finds it isn't out.

Liam (*grabbing her hand and squeezing it hard*) You tryin' to make a 'lig' out of me.

Nuala (*crying out*) You're too rough. (*Breaking away and mocking.*) Sweet sixteen and never been kissed.

He runs after and grabs her. She struggles, giggling.

(*Stopping struggling.*) What are you tryin' to do?

The Buck Lep God, you're makin' an awful job of that, boy! (*Rising.*) Desperate altogether. (*He winks at* NUALA.)

LIAM *goes behind the counter quickly.* NUALA *haughtily walks to the record player and shuffles through some records.*

Bottle of stout, kid.

LIAM *clumsily pours the drink.*

Didn't anybody ever learn you how to pour a bottle. (*Jumping back from the counter.*) For Christ's sake, the place is swimmin' in it! Bloody desperate altogether.

Liam What are you slabberin' about now, Buck Lep!

The Buck Lep (*going behind the counter, quietly*) What did you say – (*He twists his arm.*) – you dyin' lookin' bastard!

Liam (*crying out*) You're hurtin' my fuckin' arm!

The Buck Lep I'll fuckin' well kill you, you cheeky lookin' 'get' you.

Nuala (*rushing over*) Stop it, youse.

THE BUCK LEP *slowly lets go of his arm and sits down.*

Dirty foul mouths.

Liam (*producing a pistol from under the counter and pointing it*) Uncle Harry!

The Buck Lep (*rising to his feet*) Put that away!

Liam (*chuckling*) You'll get a pistol whippin'.

NUALA *gently takes the pistol from him and puts it back under the counter.*

The Buck Lep You're still shitein' yellow, kid.

Nuala That's enough of that.

LIAM *leans over the counter with his head in his hands.*

NUALA *puts on a record.*

The Buck Lep (*shouting*) Turn it down, Nuala. (*Listening.*) Jesus, that's desperate!

He turns the paper to the racing page, studies it, and marks it here and there.

Nuala (*turning off the record*) Satisfied!

The Buck Lep (*looking up from the newspaper*) 'Three Legs' got to the winnin' post last night . . . after they sent out a man with a lamp to look for it.

Liam Think I'm a fool. Youse are all very smart . . . when somebody else is doin' the dyin'.

The Buck Lep Came here to shower my head.

ROSALEEN ENTERS.

Nuala Vodka and orange, Liam.

Liam Are we callous, Rosaleen? Remember my wee cousin –

Nuala Liam . . . this is supposed to be a social club.

Liam He was machine-gunned by an assassination squad . . . don't forget. I cried hard when I saw the puddin's hangin' out of him. It was a good ceremony . . . wasn't it? That's a good stone asterick above his grave. I'll go there and cry when the war is over . . . if I'm still able.

ROSALEEN *grabs his hand and shakes it.*

The Buck Lep Always some bloody excuse. (*Referring to the newspaper.*) They say here that all the greyhounds are nervous with the shootin's and the bombin's. Christ! Give them all tranquillisers, put the hounds in wheelchairs and carry the bloody hare on a stretcher.

ROSALEEN *shakes with silent laughter.*

Holy Jesus, signs of life!

Nuala That's not fair.

The Buck Lep Well, I done it. (*To* ROSALEEN.) Go on, that's the girl.

NUALA bursts out laughing and is joined by THE BUCK LEP.

Liam Every oul' doll in this district has waited for their deliverance. It was forecast that a man on a white horse would appear in 'Pound Loney'. He would twirl his pike three times about his head and start a fire storm over the city – all that is wood is charcoal, all that is steel is twisted, all that is stone is cracked.

He looks at them a moment before pulling a piece of paper out of his pocket.

Did you hear this yet.

Singing to the tune of 'The Next Market Day'.

'Were you in Belfast when the flames
roared high,
When the Green, White and Orange
lit up the night sky.
The Falls and the Ardoyne wrote their
answer that night,
And gave the World's Press a
new tourist sight.

So click all your cameras and load
all your guns.
Slow death by the ballot box has
been outrun.
On Monday we fought for one man,
one vote,
But on Tuesday look out for your
lily-white throat.'

ROSALEEN *applauds.*

Nuala Shoo, listen! (*Armoured cars approach and pass.*)

Liam (*fiddling with the knobs of a radio receiver*) Scrambled!

Nuala They still sound excited.

The Buck Lep Who's on top of the wanted list?

Nuala Joe.

The Buck Lep Who?

Nuala That fella out of our street . . . the one that wears all them trendy ties.

Liam They'll never get him.

Nuala Will they hurt him.

The Buck Lep Who for Jesus sake!

Nuala Whoever was caught?

Liam They'll never catch him, Buck Lep.

The Buck Lep (*to* NUALA) Did I say anybody was caught!

Liam That's the spirit.

The Buck Lep Who the hell was talkin' to you! You just mind the bar.

Nuala It's like a morgue in here.

The Buck Lep (*to* LIAM) Another bottle of stout there.

Nuala God, we're all goin' to drown in a sea of alcohol!

The Buck Lep Says here in the paper – a son crowned his mother with the fryin' pan and killed her, because she objected to him gettin' married that mornin'. The father, who was stone deaf, didn't hear one word said nor blow struck. So, anyhow, later he picks up the fryin' pan with the death-dent in it . . . and fries his usual bacon and eggs.

Nuala Here . . . in Belfast!

The Buck Lep Have you got the head staggers or something! Was across the water in England. Jesus, we're not lunatics . . . it's all political here.

Liam (*cheering*) Go on, Buck Lep.

The Buck Lep Who was talkin' to you. (*He studies the racing paper.*)

Nuala It would sicken you. Can't go to the cinema because there might be a bomb. Can't go up the street to the dance hall because they're makin' them there. Can't go home because they're always rantin' the Rosary. Can't stay here because it's all murder murmurs.

Liam Accept it –

Nuala God, what!

Liam We're the 'Last of the Mohicans'. The Protestants are after us. The Army is after us. Dublin is embarrassed with us. Nobody wants us. To hell with them all!

The Buck Lep Bottle of stout, I said.

LIAM *pours the drink and puts it on the table in front of him.*

(*Grabbing him by the lapels.*) When I ask for a drink I don't want to wait ten minutes. (*Shaking him.*) Do you hear? (*Shaking him.*) Is this a bar or the city cemetery!

Nuala Leave him alone, Buck Lep.

The Buck Lep (*shaking him*) He's a brat with a brass neck.

LIAM *breaks into tears.*

Nuala (*menacingly*) You better leave him alone.

The Buck Lep If I'd left him alone when his father died where would he be now? Sure, I knew him when he could fit into an orange box.

He pushes him. LIAM *falls on the floor.*

Nuala The fruit might be sour but we don't want it bruised . . . not by our own.

The Buck Lep I was only tryin' to save his life, Nuala.

She looks at him a moment before going to LIAM *who is desperately trying to wipe the tears from his eyes.*

Nuala Try and be brave, Liam. The first light of Doomsday hasn't cracked the sky yet. The crows are still asleep – Oh God, now you have me at it. I feel like a hundred years old. Let's have a record quick. (*At the record player.*) Here's one old enough for The Buck Lep.

'The Tennessee Waltz' starts to play.

NUALA *pulls* LIAM *on to the floor to dance.*

THE BUCK LEP *watches them, as he raises his cap and scratches his head with one hand, before going to* ROSALEEN *and dancing with her.*

Liam Watch you don't fall, Buck Lep.
The Buck Lep Reminds me of my youth in Heidleberg.

They dance on until SADIE *enters out of breath.*

Sadie They've got him –! Joe's been lifted. (*They stare at her.*) The fuckin' Brits have got him. (*Cynically.*) Oh, excuse me! (*To* LIAM.) You're wanted at Battalion Headquarters.

LIAM *sticks the pistol in his belt and rushes out.*

Nuala Why did you have to spoil it for, Mrs Quinn.

She rushes forward and turns the record up very loudly.

SADIE *stares at them with her mouth open.*

SCENE 4

The factory. Early morning. ROSALEEN *works her machine. Pop music plays gently in the background.*

JIM *wheels his trolley to her bench and loads it without saying anything. He hesitates and is about to say something but changes his mind and departs.*

ROSALEEN *looks up to find him hovering near the bench again.*

Jim There's ah . . . ah – (*Roughly.*) Well, there's goin' to be a two-minute silence for them two Protestants killed by your bomb yesterday. All fenians will stand to attention or there'll be trouble.

He leaves as NUALA *approaches.*

Nuala (*noticing the pain on* ROSALEEN's *face*) What did he say? (*Shouting after him.*) Commere, you shifty-eyed, whoor's after-birth you!
Jim (*approaching and pointing to himself*) Me?
Nuala Yes you, you shite. What did you say to Rosaleen?
Jim Nothing.
Nuala You did. I'm not cabbage lookin' . . . am I?

Jim Ask her.

Nuala (*pushing the trolley*) Get away from here!

Jim (*as he is leaving*) You'll stand the two-minute silence . . . straight as rhubarb stalks.

Nuala (*running towards him and pushing the trolley*) I'll –

Helen (*appearing suddenly*) Up here again, Quigley?

Nuala We're being annoyed.

Helen Oh! How's that?

Nuala Is there goin' to be a two-minute silence here?

Helen That's a matter for the shop steward.

Nuala When was the meetin'?

Helen How do I know!

Nuala It was held away from the factory last night?

Helen (*mock surprise*) Oh, weren't you invited! I wonder why?

Nuala It's a misuse of the Trade Union.

Helen Some of us are of the opinion, around here, that it's been misused too often – like that withdrawal of labour for the pay rise. I didn't notice you breakin' the strike . . . you held out your hand like the rest of them here – Anyhow, there's goin' to be a tribute paid to the dead this afternoon.

Nuala I'll keep the silence but I'll be sayin' a few 'Hail Marys' to myself.

Helen Please yourself whatever way you want to communicate with the devil.

> *As she starts to walk away . . .*

Nuala Commere you . . . I want you.

Helen (*turning quickly*) Yes!

Nuala I'll report you.

Helen (*cynically*) To your friends?

Nuala The Public Protection Bureau.

Helen Isn't it sad you can't tell Willie Whitelaw as well.

Nuala (*pointing to* ROSALEEN) I have a witness.

Helen That 'stone'! Don't make me laugh.

> NUALA *quickly picks up a hammer from the bench and advances on her.*

(*Sternly.*) Put that hammer down!

> JIM *comes running.*

(*To* JIM.) Get about your work, you lazy 'get'! (*She walks away quickly.*)

Jim (*shouting after her*) There'll be another bloody strike if you don't watch yourself! Bitch has been persecutin' me all mornin'. She was even waitin' outside the shitehouse while I made my water.

Nuala (*sticking her nose in the air*) We don't wish to hear talk like that.

Jim It's too bloody much. I had a time of it last night. My oul' da was drunk again to belt bustin'. Smashed the delph-dog, then lets the pigeons out and starts shootin' at them with his point twenty-two. The police and army were round. He got away lucky. It'll be the 'Battle of the Boyne' again tonight . . . for my oul' doll'll get him when he's broke and sober.

Nuala (*closing her eyes*) Hmmmph! (*To* ROSALEEN, *indicating* JIM.) He's rough.

Jim What was the supervisor sayin'?

Nuala She said she'd trail the hair out of me if I didn't get back to my bench – Didn't she, Rosaleen? That's when I lifted the hammer.

Jim This Helen Shaw's gone 'off the square' altogether. Report her to the shop steward.

Nuala I will . . . when I calm down.

Jim I wouldn't put up with that. Definitely got to stick together. Oh definitely! (*Mumbling to himself as he leaves.*) Ay . . . definitely.

Nuala I know you're standin' there puttin' silent judgements on us all. God, even a stone weeps sometimes! Oh . . . I don't feel myself today. That reminds me. I heard that Helen Shaw's boyfriend is a soldier. Somebody saw them wrapped round each other at the Candlelight Coffee House. His short haircut and English accent gave it away. She denied it – Probably afraid he'd be tracked . . . don't blame her – Oh God, I better get back to my bench.

She points her nose in the air and goes as HELEN *approaches.*

Helen There's been complaints. (*Taking a piece of metal from her bench and examining it closely.*) I can't see what's wrong with this. (*Looking up the factory.*) What are they talking about in the Inspection Room! Look, just stand your ground when the two-minute silence comes. Don't move . . . it won't take long. My father was a socialist – Well, he was more than that. When they had the two-minute silence in the shipyards for the late King George the Sixth, he talked all through it. 'There was mammy bear, and daddy bear, and wee pink-bummed baby bear – (*In a gruff voice while shaking her head.*) What a fairy story!' He thought they were going to kill him afterwards . . . and he was a Protestant. We were still laughing about it years later. Maybe in time to come we'll laugh about this . . . and we'll just be bursting with the tears running down our. faces.

JIM *approaches.*

Yes, what do you want?

Jim You're to come quick, Miss Shaw. Old Mrs O'Kane has taken bad in the canteen again.

Helen She's just had another turn, Jim.

She leaves quickly.

Jim (*to himself*) Jim! I don't understand the woman. And there she's gone off to attend to one of your tribe . . . she'd play step-mother to the Pope. (*Moving away.*) I don't want Helen to find me here . . . the bitch.

ROSALEEN *works until the machine and music noises die away and the lunch-time hooter blows.*

NUALA *appears carrying two cups of tea. They sit on the bench eating sandwiches.*

Nuala Is everything all set for you goin' to your father's grave at Milltown on Sunday? (*More to herself.*) Of course it is – Where's that Jim Sloane? (*Looking cautiously down the factory.*) That's funny! Mrs O'Kane promised to go to the Out-Patient's this afternoon. (*Looking down the factory again.*) He's not wanted up here . . . anyway, let him sit with his own kind. (*Picking up a magazine.*) I'm fed-up talkin' to a brick wall.

ROSALEEN *picks up a book and starts reading.*

What's that –? Oh, never mind. I'm goin' to the Rest Room. (*She leaves.*)

HELEN *approaches followed by* JIM. ROSALEEN *gives her a slight smile.*

Helen Hope we're givin' you plenty to do, McGurk! (*To* JIM.) Put them up quick before that English manager comes back. Once they're up he'll cause a riot if he orders them down. Now be quick and don't you tell who told you . . . I have my instructions, too.

JIM *hesitates before pulling the Ulster Red Hand flag from beneath his jacket. He hesitates again while looking at* ROSALEEN.

Where's your guts! Some leader, some Shower of Hail! Never mind her. (*Hushed tones.*) Quickly. (*She walks away.*)

JIM *whistles, embarrassed, as he sets about nailing up the flags.*

Jim Hey, Rosaleen, hold the end of this flag till I put a nail in it.

She holds it while he nails. Suddenly, he hits his thumb.

(*Dancing around, squeezing his thumb and blowing on it.*) Christ, I've mashed myself! It's your fault. I wouldn't have to do this only for you.

(*He grabs the hammer and hurls it across the floor.*) Fenians!

Helen (*approaching*) Finished? (*Catching sight of* ROSALEEN *holding the flag.*) Let go of that flag! Trying to make fools out of us?

She drops the flag.

(*Grabbing it and dusting it.*) You let it fall in the dust deliberately. (*To* JIM *who is still blowing and sucking his thumb.*) Didn't she? (*Watching him a moment.*) I can see now why you only drag a trolley around this factory. We'd be signing your death warrant by putting you on a machine. (*Pushing him.*) Get out of my road. (*She grabs the hammer and nails up the flag.*) My father must be turning in his bloody grave! (*To* ROSALEEN.) That's not for your ears.

The back-to-work hooter goes.

Quick, it's near time.

The music and factory sounds go on.

As ROSALEEN *approaches her machine the power is cut off and the music dies away.*

NUALA *appears silently.*

What! Back here again, Quigley?

NUALA *doesn't say anything but stands silently beside* ROSALEEN.

Watch them, Jim. (*Studying her watch a moment before jumping to attention.*) Now!

JIM *jumps to attention. The hooter blows one long blast. They stand silently.*

ROSALEEN *starts to rock on her heels and collapses on the floor. 'The Queen' starts playing.*

Nuala (*beside her*) Rosaleen!

HELEN *and* JIM *wait until the hooter blasts before running to her.*

Helen (*feeling her pulse*) She's only fainted.
Nuala What did Rosaleen ever do to you, Miss Shaw?
Helen (*agitated*) Nothing, nothing –!
Jim They broke the silence.
Helen (*standing up*) Yes, that's what you have done.
Jim (*looking up the factory*) There'll be an investigation.
Helen (*alarmed as she follows his gaze*) Will there! If I were you two I'd leave the factory right now . . . till things calm down.
Nuala Aren't you even goin' to let her have a glass of water?
Helen (*to* JIM) Get some water, quick!

ROSALEEN *recovers. They both make her comfortable.*

Nuala Feelin' better?
Helen I can't make head or tail of you two.
Nuala Or us of you, Miss Shaw. Peculiar . . . Rosaleen hasn't spoken for four years, yet, I know how she feels and thinks.
Helen What way –? (*Harshly.*) It's no use . . . I'm angry.

JIM *arrives with the glass of water.* HELEN *gives* ROSALEEN *the water. She rises.* NUALA *helps her on with her coat.*

They both leave without looking at HELEN *or* JIM.

It's a pity of them.

Jim They should never have been allowed in here to work.

HELEN *doesn't answer.*

I'm gettin' the gang together again tonight, Helen.

Helen (*sharply*) Get your trolley and clear that bench. There's too much slackness around here.

She goes leaving JIM *looking bewildered.*

SCENE 5

A Sunday afternoon in Milltown Cemetery.

A squat, stone monument topped by a stone angel. A chiselled inscription reads:

**CAPTAIN SEAN McGURK 'C' COMPANY
KILLED IN ACTION 4 JULY 1957**

Nearby another monument with a worn inscription partly reads:

MURDERED – 1892

ROSALEEN *and* MATILDA, *wearing mass mantillas, tend the grave – plucking out weeds, cutting the mangy grass with scissors, arranging bunches of flowers in the stone vases, placing the photographs of* ROSALEEN *as a child, and another of* MATILDA *and* SEAN *on their wedding day, against the monument. Now and again* MATILDA *sprinkles holy water, from a medicine bottle, over the grave.*

After they have finished their tasks, they both kneel and tell their rosary beads.

ROSALEEN *crosses herself, rises, and wanders over to the old monument.*

An army helicopter passes slowly overhead.

Matilda (*looking into the grave*) Hear me . . . you without ears. Listen! Through the spokes of your bones. Look! . . . up at your greasy-red sky without moon, sun or stars. (*Rising exasperated.*) I am over here . . . standin' in a cobwebbed corner of the world. Too close to Justice, so far from Mercy. (*Hushed tones.*) I saw the 'peeler' who done it. They say your lead's in him still . . . I wouldn't wonder. Stumblin' about like a rogue bullock with a chained log hangin' from his neck. Even the pity of it all is starting to leave me . . . you suffer to save up the years and it's only minutes of wet tears over a cold grave in the end. (*Turning her head away.*) They sent you well away that day . . . after the speech by the man in the shabby Burton suit . . . the flags of the colour party, the rosary in Irish, the guns sayin' goodbye across this blighted patch, markin' time on December ground . . . I'm left . . . woven into a tradition that won't die without me.

ROSALEEN *hovers near.*

Your wee girl is here . . . silent as mercury behind glass.

Sounds drift over from a nearby burial party. ROSALEEN *quickly clutches at* MATILDA.

1st Voice Requiescent in pace. Amen.

Matilda Merciful God, another one!

2nd Voice (*partially heard as the wind changes*) Gathered here . . . graveside . . . young Irish soldier . . . killed in action . . . Crown Forces . . . noblest cause . . . Ireland . . . Remains . . . seventeen year old . . . death . . . be avenged . . . blood . . . Volunteer Rory –

A bugle blows.

3rd Voice (*sharply*) Ready . . . Aim . . . Fire!

A volley of shots crack across the cemetery.

A discordant rendering of 'A Soldier's Song' plays on a portable record player. Then there is silence.

Matilda (*revolving the wedding ring on her finger*) High Street . . . Saturday afternoon . . . a plastic bag of a day . . . spendin' the bonus and the overtime. Searchin' for the metal that would ring me like a rare exotic bird – No, it wasn't like that. There was love – But love forges the strongest prison bars of all. No, it wasn't like that either. It was intensity. It was the struggle of the tide to fill the shore before it leaves quietly with its head down. (*Agonizingly.*) Oh God!

She takes off the wedding ring and places it on the grave.

Goodbye, Sean. I'll try not to hear you anymore.

She picks up the photographs and walks away.

ROSALEEN *kneels and puts her ear against the grave, listening.*
The army helicopter passes slowly overhead again.

SCENE 6

Early in the morning at the MCGURK's *home.* MATILDA *enters in a dressing-gown. She hesitates before shaking the flask on the table. She freezes as she finds it half empty. She examines the cup and saucer and a partially eaten sandwich. She hides everything quickly.* NUALA *knocks and enters.*

Nuala Bad night last night. I counted two hundred and twelve shots. They must have been after the army post.

Matilda (*setting the table*) Yes.

Nuala Is Rosaleen ready?

Matilda Oh, was she to go in today?

Nuala Yes, everything is all right at the factory again.

Matilda I'll get her down. (*She goes.*)

> *A knock on the door and* THE BUCK LEP *enters with a bricklayer's spirit level in his hand.*

The Buck Lep Here I am – faithful guardian. Walk youse to work.

Nuala Who's protectin' who?

The Buck Lep Absolute murder last night. Troops'll be pickin' up lone males, I reckon. Can't afford to lose a day's wages – five bread-snatchers and a wife – In case you don't know.

Nuala You're safe with us, Buck Lep.

The Buck Lep (*looking at the spirit level*) Wish they'd make these things to fold. Troops might think it's something else. They're a bit nervous this mornin'.

Matilda (*entering with* ROSALEEN) Nice mornin' that, Buck Lep.

The Buck Lep I think it'll hold up well today, Matilda.

Matilda Sit down all of youse and I'll get the kettle on. (*She goes.*)

Nuala (*switching on the radio, she sways and snaps her fingers to the music*) I don't think that'll make it. (*She turns down the radio.*)

The Buck Lep I've a nice wee job for today – brickin' up a few burnt houses near Library Street . . . and there's a bookies just round the corner. I fancy 'Runnin' Wild' today.

Nuala We don't go in for horse racin'.

The Buck Lep Fancy runnin' wild today, Nuala?

Nuala (*to* ROSALEEN) Listen to him – oul' married man!

The Buck Lep In that case I'll have to wait till pay night.

Nuala The wife's got you taped – no wage packet, no love.

The Buck Lep Constant 'Battle of the Bulge', Nuala.

Nuala Too early in the mornin' for that talk.

Matilda (*entering and pouring the tea*) Have any of youse seen young Liam this mornin'?

> *They look at her a moment without saying anything.*

The Buck Lep He'll be in the district somewhere.

Matilda Is he safe?

Nuala There's no reason why he shouldn't be, Mrs McGurk.

The Buck Lep Nobody was hit last night . . . it was successful.

Matilda Successful?

The Buck Lep I can't think of any other word. Failure is no use either . . . there's no word in between.

Matilda There's something not makin' sense to me anymore.

> *A knock on the door.*

Nuala I'd keep quiet about it if I were you, Mrs McGurk.

The Buck Lep You do that, Matilda.

Sadie (*entering*) Do you mind if I come in, Matilda?

Matilda Come on ahead, Sadie. What's all the ceremony about all of a sudden.

Sadie When youse are ready I'll walk down part of the way.

The Buck Lep I'm startin' to feel safer already.

Sadie Not if you'd been in our street at dawn. The Brits searched high and they searched low. Our floorboards have been taken up that often they're like matchwood . . . we've stopped nailin' them down again . . . and, I'm thinkin' of gettin' see-through settees and mattress'. It was a good thing that my Liam was at his auntie's in Andersonstown for the night . . . he would have been awful upset –

The Buck Lep Shouldn't we start to dander down –

Sadie They were fired on comin' out of the houses and that sent them searchin' again.

Nuala Was anything found?

Sadie Hairpins, a broken comb and three old pennies.

A short burst of automatic fire nearby.

The Buck Lep Wait till you hear.

Dustbin lids bang, whistles blow and a portable fog horn moans.

Armoured cars enter the street amid shouted orders.

The door is banged and the SOLDIER *enters.*

Soldier (*pointing his rifle*) Do YOU all live here?

Matilda I live here with my daughter.

Soldier Names?

Matilda Matilda and Rosaleen McGurk.

Soldier (*going towards the black-draped photo*) We have that.

ROSALEEN *springs between the photo and the* SOLDIER.

MATILDA *gently leads* ROSALEEN *to a chair.*

(*Pointing.*) You?

Nuala Nuala Quigley . . . number twenty-seven along the street.

Soldier (*to* SADIE) Hallo again. (*Into street.*) Mrs Quinn, number three Rose Street.

An army radio crackles with incoherent speech.

Sadie Youse have already searched us . . . thanks very much.

Soldier What are you doin' up here?

Sadie Some of us have to work.

Soldier Where's that?

Sadie Twentieth Century Fashions.

Soldier You, sir, stand up.

The Buck Lep (*standing up*) Will this take long?

Soldier (*searching him with one hand*) Name?

The Buck Lep The Buck Lep

Soldier Do me a favour!

The Buck Lep Harry.

Soldier What?

The Buck Lep Smith.

Soldier That name don't belong to this district.

The Buck Lep I'm not an O'Flynn or an O'Brien . . . if that's what you mean.

Soldier What was that first name again?

The Buck Lep The Buck Lep – cap. (*Touching the peak of his cap in mock salute.*) Get it . . . me old cock sparrow?

Soldier Right! (*Pointing to the spirit level.*) What's this?

The Buck Lep A spirit level for bricklayin'.

Soldier (*taking it and hitting it hard on the floor*) Sure?

The Buck Lep You'll put it out of true . . . it cost five pounds fifty.

Soldier (*looking through the bubble*) Couldn't see much with this on a dark night.

The Buck Lep We don't work much at night.

Soldier Day Unit?

The Buck Lep (*imitating his accent*) Wha's yo're gime, eh?

Soldier Fifty-four across the street?

The Buck Lep I suppose so.

Soldier Why was your door not locked last night?

The Buck Lep I slipped out to get a packet of 'fegs'.

Soldier 'Curly Face' was closed last night.

The Buck Lep Borrowed some from a mate.

Soldier Which mate?

The Buck Lep Don't remember.

Soldier Have to.

The Buck Lep No . . . won't.

Soldier (*picking up the spirit level*) I arrest you under paragraph five, clause six of the Special Powers Act.

Matilda Don't take him, soldier, he's got five childer –

Sadie (*to* MATILDA, *angrily*) Get off your bloody knees! (*To* SOLDIER.) You rat-fuckin'-faced bastard! (*She pounds him with her fists and spits in his face.*)

Soldier (*throwing her backwards on to the floor*) Do you want to come as well, you bleedin' bitch.

The Buck Lep (*rushing forward to pick her up*) For Christ's sake, Sadie!

Soldier (*pointing his rifle at him*) Oy! Come along. (*Into street.*) Another one for 'Q-One' here.

THE BUCK LEP *cautiously leaves with his hands on his head followed by the* SOLDIER.

Matilda (*into street*) He's done nothing!

Sadie (*looking long and hard at her*) That's the trouble.

Nuala I feel shaky all over.

Matilda Sit down, Nuala.

Nuala We'll be late for work.

Matilda I'm sure they'll understand.

Sadie (*cynically*) Isn't that just great!

Nuala A whole week off, but, at least we'll be paid . . . thanks to the manager.

Sadie (*to* NUALA) You're easily bought.

Matilda Leave her alone now . . . can't you see the girl is worried and nervous.

Nuala I live a minute at a time now . . . I just go into a dream . . . someday I'll wake up and the trouble will be all over.

> ROSALEEN, *who has been watching the proceedings quietly without emotion, comes forward to hold* NUALA's *hand.*

Matilda Let's hope you're not my age when you do, Nuala.

Voice (*from the street*) They've arrested The Buck Lep!

> *Sounds of a riot outside – people shouting, the occasional ragged bang of a rubber-bullet gun, metal bouncing off concrete and glass breaking.*

Matilda God, I wish *I* was a heathen worshipin' Mars!

Sadie Isn't it great the way the whole district's heard about The Buck Lep's arrest already.

Matilda (*more to herself*) Now's the time to calm down and think.

Sadie (*angrily*) It's all right for you! (*Pointing to the photo.*) You have a dead republican to protect you.

Matilda Who from?

Sadie From us.

Nuala Mrs Quinn!

Matilda Let her have her say, Nuala.

Sadie No, it's you I want to hear.

Nuala The stones have stopped.

Sadie (*going closer to her*) What IS your opinion of us?

Nuala We best be gettin' to work.

Matilda It must be the end of something . . . don't quite know what yet. I'll still have to go through the movements of the old tradition . . . for there's no safe niche upon the face of the earth for me now. (*Painfully.*) Ooooh! (*Recovering.*) I'll phone about The Buck Lep before I go and comfort his wife.

Sadie I knew Sean was watchin' over you . . . despite yourself.

Matilda (*turning down her collar*) Thank God the world is full of foreigners! How could we attempt any change if we all were neighbours.

> SADIE *looks at her fiercely before departing.*

SCENE 7

A few minutes before lunch-time. The factory is heavily decorated with Ulster Red Hand flags, and red, white and blue bunting.

ROSALEEN *works at her bench a while before* HELEN *approaches to examine her work.*

Helen Hope you had a nice rest. What I had to put up with was nobody's business. Shop-floor meetings . . . two one-hour token strikes. They even brought in a pipe band to re-dedicate the factory. They demanded both your dismissals. I put my foot down there. When they finally started to swear and tell dirty jokes I knew things had returned to normal.

The hooter blows.

All right now? (*She exits.*)

Nuala (*approaching with two cups of tea*) Can't you even go and get the tea sometimes – I'm sorry.

They both sit on the bench and unwrap their sandwiches. NUALA *is silent.* ROSALEEN *continually looks at her, expecting her to talk.*

JIM *approaches slowly dragging his trolley with a cup of tea balanced on it. He sits down on the trolley some distance from them and opens his lunch tin. He doesn't look at them but eats silently.*

(*Pretending not to notice him.*) He behaved himself all mornin'.

JIM *doesn't answer.*

Miss Shaw might put him on a machine yet.

Jim (*wearily*) Is that me you're talkin' about, girl.

Nuala (*pretending to see him for the first time*) I should have known – 'Careless talk costs lives'!

Jim (*quietly*) You sound just like my oul' da . . . always on about the North Atlantic run. You'd think it was just him and Hitler in the last war. 'We had wooden ships and iron men, now it's iron ships and wooden men.'

Nuala (*to* ROSALEEN) He looks like an old man's child . . . all puckered at the seams.

Jim Stop it, Nuala.

Nuala Hmmph! (*She looks from* JIM *to* ROSALEEN *and back again, embarrassed.*)

Jim Your Mrs O'Kane will never come back here to work.

Nuala (*to* ROSALEEN) Cancer.

Jim (*drawing his trolley closer*) She spent the last week in hospital.

Nuala (*to* ROSALEEN) She's been sent home to die.

Jim (*drawing his trolley closer*) We only heard about it this mornin'.

Nuala (*to* ROSALEEN) She wants to try for a miracle in Lourdes.

Jim The Shop Steward Committee's meetin' about it now.

Nuala Will they help, Jim?

Jim (*rising and going close to them*) They're fairly decent.

Helen (*approaching and beckoning*) Jim.

Jim Excuse me a wee moment.

> *He exits with* HELEN.

Nuala One blow for peace, two kicks for war. Oh, I mus'n't think like this. I'll be ruined before forty if I do. Say something, Rosaleen, and help me. Wish I could be silent . . . like a wall. Oh, I'd be supportin' the roof. Why can't I be the roof sometimes. Maybe I'd like to be a dog – No, that would be no good either. They'd call me Seamus or they'd call me William. William would chase the nuns and Seamus would howl at Orange pipe music. What about a bee? A bee's a hard worker. That would be no good either. A bee can be blown up too . . . like them scorched bees lyin' on the ground in Falls Park. I'm tired. I want to go into hibernation and wait for eternity.

> ROSALEEN *reaches out and holds her hand.*

Jim (*approaching, embarrassed*) I haven't spoilt it.

> *He takes a collecting tin from behind his back with a Union Jack label on it.*

> (*Looking at it.*) It was the first tin that came to hand. But wait till I tell youse. (*Shaking the tin.*) It's been agreed . . . every worker pledged to pay fifty pence. (*Shaking the tin.*) Hear that! Won't be long till your oul' Mrs O'Kane's on her way to the Vatican –

Nuala Lourdes!

Jim She might even catch sight of the Pope havin' a paddle in holy water.

Nuala Or the Queen, wearin' a red petticoat, jumpin' from rock to rock, screechin' 'Irish!'.

Jim Ay, that could happen as well.

Nuala (*softly*) Commere . . . closer. (*Winking at* ROSALEEN, *she kisses him on the cheek and bursts out laughing.*)

Jim (*embarrassed*) You're goin' to spoil me.

> *She makes a sign indicating* ROSALEEN. JIM *quietly kisses her on the cheek.*

Nuala We better keep an eye on him . . . wild man.

> *They both take coins from their pockets and drop them into the tin.*

Jim Wait a minute till I catch the rest of them. (*Calling out as he goes.*) Don't think, give with your hearts!

Nuala I can't stand anymore. (*She grabs hold of* ROSALEEN *and starts to scream and cry. She runs away still crying.*)

> JIM *comes back pulling his trolley.* NUALA *stands on it laughing – near to hysteria.*

Jim Hold on, hold on!

Nuala Yoo hoo, yoo hoo!

> *The return-to-work hooter blows. Music and machines start up. He draws the trolley close to* ROSALEEN'S *bench and starts to load it.*

Jim Would youse like to come down to Billy McKeown's Bar some week-end? Ballywalter . . . neutral territory.

Nuala We're not great drinkers.

Jim There's a disco in the back room.

Nuala (*mocking*) On the back of your bike!

Jim My mate's got a car. We could pick youse up at the Candlelight . . . that would be safe. Comin'?

Nuala We'd have to think it over.

Jim There are all kinds there.

Nuala (*to* ROSALEEN) What do you think?

Jim Never any bother. Comin'?

Nuala We'll let you know.

Jim Sure?

Nuala Ay, we'll let you know.

Helen's Voice Jim Sloane! (*He exits quickly.*)

Nuala Would you risk it? (ROSALEEN *desperately tries to say something.*) We'll accept then. Don't tell him too soon. Stop lookin' so excited – He's back.

Jim (*rushing in and grabbing his trolley*) Get out! There's a bomb in the factory! (*Shouting as he pulls his trolley.*) Come on, don't stand there – ! Make for the waste ground!

Helen (*running in tight-lipped and breaking his grip on the trolley*) Leave it!

> JIM *pulls* ROSALEEN *by the sleeve and they all exit hurriedly.*

> *The factory is empty. The music and machine noises continue.*

> *After some time the* SOLDIER *enters cautiously with a long coil of rope over his shoulder.*

Soldier (*into radio*) Cut the power.

> *The noise stops. The main lights go out. The* SOLDIER *stands very still in the half-gloom before starting to swivel very slowly, listening, and looking through the telescopic sight of his rifle at the factory.*

> (*Into radio, in hushed tones.*) Suspected object in sight.

> *He uncoils the rope and disappears.*

> *He re-appears, after some time, crawling on his stomach with the end of the rope in his hands. He throws it off-stage.*

> (*Into radio.*) Now slow . . . slow, slow . . . slow – It's a bloody big bastard.

> *A packing case comes into sight. He crawls forward to steady it.*

Baby, we can't keep meeting like this. Slow . . . slow, slow . . . slow –

The rope jerks and the packing case almost falls over.

(*Shouting.*) Bastards! (*He flattens himself on the ground and covers his head with his hands.*)

(*Steadying it.*) Slow . . . don't put your mutton out of joint. Slow – (*As it disappears he blows it a kiss.*)

He dives under ROSALEEN's *bench and lies flat.*

He waits until he hears a loud cheer before raising his head.

Voice (*from radio*) Bomb cleared . . . another fucking hoax . . . over and out.

He stands up and leans on the bench as a wave of sickness comes over him.

He lights a cigarette as the power comes on again.

ROSALEEN *and* NUALA *enter cautiously.*

Soldier It's all over – Don't be afraid. (*Stretching out his hands.*) Look at my hands! (*He waits for some response.*) Nice cup of tea would go down well. (*They don't respond.*) Where's the canteen? (NUALA *points.*) Cup of tea? (*They don't answer.*) I'll check on it. (*He goes.*)

Nuala (*fearfully*) Here's Helen. (*As she approaches.*) It wasn't our fault, Miss Shaw –

Helen (*quietly*) Where's that soldier gone? (ROSALEEN *points.*) He mus'n't know that I work in a place like this. (*Rushing away.*) Tell me when he's gone.

Nuala (*looking a moment at* ROSALEEN) Now I get it! They were the cuties seen in the Candlelight. Wait till I see Lizzie. (*She exits.*)

Soldier (*approaching with three cups of tea on a tray*) Where's your mate? (*He waits for a reply.*) Still shocked? Here drink.

Jim (*approaching*) Good job you done there, fella.

Soldier (*exaggerated sweep of his hands*) Nothing to it, mate . . . do it all the time. (*To* ROSALEEN.) Put plenty of sugar into it . . . good for shock.

Soldier (*nudging him*) Deaf and dumb . . . eh?

Jim Be careful what you say . . . she could hear the bloody grass growin'.

NUALA *approaches and whispers in* ROSALEEN's *ear. They both look at the* SOLDIER *and smile.*

Am I missin' something?

Soldier Don't try to understand them, boy.

Jim I'm startin' to think the same myself.

Nuala (*coaxingly*) Jim.

JIM *moves away and stares at them.*

Soldier Miss Shaw around?

Nuala (*tittering and holding her hand to her mouth*) She was sent to the other factory.

Soldier Have I seen you somewhere before. (*To* ROSALEEN.) You too?

Jim Up the Falls where they play 'tig' with hatchets.

Nuala (*to* SOLDIER) Been there?

Jim (*to* SOLDIER) Say nothing . . . not to 'them'.

Nuala We're 'us' and you're 'them'.

Jim That's were you're wrong, girl. We're 'us' and you're 'them'.

Nuala No, you shite! We're 'us', you're 'them'.

Soldier (*finishing his tea*) Nice cup of tea that.

Nuala (*to* SOLDIER) Ask him what he's got around his neck.

Jim (*moving away as he puts his hand to his chest*) It's only a souvenir. (*He exits.*)

Soldier Let's break it up. Cheers. (*He exits.*)

Nuala Showin' us up in front of the Brit . . . so he was – Oh Jesus! He's the one that arrested The Buck Lep.

Helen (*approaching*) Thank God he's gone!

Jim (*entering quickly*) Miss Shaw! The Security Committee is about to meet.

Helen (*agitated, to* NUALA) Go!

Nuala (*desperately*) Is it very far to Ballywalter, Jim.

Jim I lost my way once but I'll not do it again.

Helen (*almost screaming*) Go . . . please!

> ROSALEEN *lifts a hammer and bangs in down loudly on the bench.*
> *They all freeze as they look at her.*

END OF ACT I

ACT II

SCENE 1

About two a.m. The MCGURK's *home is dark except for the burning red of the Sacred Heart lamp.*

The sound of automatic fire breaks across the city. The sounds get nearer, mingled with the screaming engines of armoured cars in nearby streets.

The sounds start to fade and only occasional shots are heard.

A lone army helicopter flies overhead beaming its powerful search-light on the houses. Neighbourhood dogs start barking.

The helicopter fades slowly . . . distant dogs bark.

Something bangs against the street door. A number of attempts are made to open the door before it finally swings open.

The groaning, huddled figure of LIAM *wearing a black beret, a khaki combat jacket and clutching a machine-gun, falls into the kitchen.*

He crawls towards the table and grabs at the flask of tea, knocking it on the floor.

ROSALEEN, *wearing a coat over her night-dress, enters fearfully before rushing to shut and bolt the street door. She approaches* LIAM *cautiously.*

Liam (*weakly*) Volunteer Liam Quinn. (ROSALEEN *bends over him.*) My gun –

> *She picks up the gun gingerly, looks around the kitchen, exits, and returns immediately.*

> (*Groaning loudly.*) Rosaleen. (*She attempts to move him.*) It's too far. (*Groaning.*) I'm finished –

> *She violently shakes her head.*

> Dyin' takes no trainin'. (*He lets out a loud moan.*)

> *She clenches her fists and raises her trembling arms to the ceiling. She lets out a long, low moan.*

Rosaleen (*pulling open his jacket and looking at his wounds*) Noooooooo!
Liam You're not Rosaleen – I'm cold.

> *She takes her coat and covers him.*

Rosaleen (*stuttering and banging the floor with her fist*) I . . . 'll . . . get . . . the . . . pri . . . est.
Liam (*grabbing her arm*) No time. (*He moans loudly.*)

> ROSALEEN *gets the medicine bottle of holy water.*

Rosaleen (*sprinkling it on his brow*) Fa . . . ther . . . Son . . . Holeee . . . Gh . . . ost . . . A . . . men.

Liam I can't cry.

Rosaleen Nor . . . me . . . for . . . give . . . me – Leee . . . am.

Liam I WANT my mammy – No, I don't.

Rosaleen Ma . . . meee . . . is . . . here.

Liam Hear my confession, Father. I stole more altar wine and never confessed.

Rosaleen Wa . . . sss . . . it . . . ni . . . ice?

Liam It made me sick, Mammy.

> *There is a moment of silence.*

Rosaleen (*shaking him*) Quick! Pr . . . ay.

Liam (*with great difficulty*) 'Oh my God! I am –

> *She holds his hand.*

– heartily sorry for all my sins – ' Put on a record.

Rosaleen Go . . . on. (*She shakes him.*)

Liam ' – For all my sins . . . because they offend Thee . . . who art infinitely . . . good . . . and I resolve . . . with the help . . . of thy grace . . . never to offend . . . Thee again.' (*She makes the sign of the cross on his forehead.*)

> *She fiddles desperately with the knobs of the radio, picking up foreign stations until an American voice comes over.*

Radio ' – Three a.m. Central European Time. Stay tuned to AFN' – (*A pop record plays.*)

Liam I can't hear. (*She turns it up.*)

Rosaleen (*stroking his forehead*) Leee . . . am.

> MATILDA *rushes into the kitchen and stares aghast, unable to move.*

> ROSALEEN *shakes him. He doesn't move or answer. She turns on the light and switches off the radio.*

Matilda (*crying out*) Liam! (*She rushes forward and slaps him on the ear.*)

Rosaleen (*grabbing her hand*) Sto . . . op!

> MATILDA *jumps back from the body.*

Ooooooh!

> MATILDA *holds her as she sobs.*

Matilda Careful, daughter! All these years were carved in stone . . . dynamited silence has a lot of shrapnel. (*Kneeling beside him, feeling his pulse, her ear close to his mouth.*) He seems dead.

> *An armoured car passes in the distance.*

Rosaleen Hi . . . ide . . . him!

Matilda (*looking at her a moment*) Do we have to?

ROSALEEN *nods her head violently.*

Are you sure?

Rosaleen (*banging the floor with her fist*) Yes!

Matilda All right. I'll ask advice off The Buck Lep.

She puts a coat over her night clothes and exits.

ROSALEEN *gets a face flannel and soap, washes his face and combs his hair. She crosses his hands across his chest . . . switches on the radio and sits down to wait.*

THE BUCK LEP *enters looking bedraggled – undone shoelaces, without socks, an overcoat over his pyjamas but wearing his cap.*

He looks in horror from ROSALEEN *to* LIAM *before being pushed into the room by* MATILDA.

The Buck Lep Are you sure he's dead.

Matilda Positive . . . now tell us what to do.

The Buck Lep Bloody young bastard . . . I told him!

Rosaleen Now!

The Buck Lep Well, ah, it's – (*He moves away from* ROSALEEN, *looking at her suspiciously.*)

Matilda For Christ's sake, Buck Lep, don't be an oul' woman!

The Buck Lep (*kneeling beside* LIAM) You've made a pig's arse of it now, boy.

Rosaleen Hur . . . eee.

The Buck Lep I think I know the place – It's shock, Rosaleen.

Rosaleen (*pulling at him*) Now!

Matilda Shouldn't his mother be brought?

An armoured car passes the end of the street.

The Buck Lep Not now.

Matilda What are you hesitatin' for now?

The Buck Lep This is not my line – (*Gritting his teeth.*) I'm not in the 'Movement' but I still nearly got a rifle-butt in the mouth while being held by Army Intelligence.

Matilda It's a neighbour's boy – God, have you no pity!

The Buck Lep Oul' Seamus is the morgue keeper for them – (*He hesitates.*)

Matilda And what!

The Buck Lep It'll be a job gettin' him there.

Matilda We'll help you . . . won't we, Rosaleen.

ROSALEEN *nods her head and utters an inarticulate sound.*

The Buck Lep Quick then, get something to wrap him in.

MATILDA *exits.*

(*Looking at her a while.*) How long has the talkin' been goin' on?

She doesn't answer but bends down takes her coat off the body and puts it on. For a moment she stands still, thinking, before going through LIAM's *pockets and taking out his Rosary Beads, a few coins and a small cash book.*

Bloody young skitter! What was HE doin' with a cash book. (*Looking over her shoulder as she thumbs through it.*) Looks like a diary of some sort.

MATILDA *returns with a blanket and spreads it on the floor.*

We'll have to hurry in case of a search.

Rosaleen (*reading*) 'Jan . . . u . . . ary . . . twen . . . twenty . . . three –

They go closer to her and watch her struggle to speak.

I . . . was . . . made . . . a . . . full . . . vol . . . un . . . teer . . . to . . . day . . .
I . . . was . . . ver . . . eee . . . proud . . . and . . . could . . . hard . . . ly . . .
re . . . peat . . . the . . . oath –' (*She stops exhausted.* MATILDA *takes the book.*)

Matilda (*reading*) 'I could hardly repeat the oath for tears –' That's very good, Rosaleen . . . isn't it, Buck Lep?

He doesn't answer.

(*Turning the page.*) The 'thirteenth of February – I lie in bed listenin' to a far-off train. It reminds me of my holidays in Carnlough with my brothers and sisters. Now I can only plan how to cripple it and watch it lyin' on its side with its guts pourin' out.
Fourteenth of February. I saw her comin' home from the factory again. Why does she pretend not to see me. She knows I like her. Does she know I am shy? She only waves when I wave first. Then she walks on –'

Rosaleen (*taking the book quickly*) 'Third . . . April . . . Thank . . . God . . . the buds . . . are . . . on . . . the trees . . . This . . . winter . . . was . . . too . . . long . . . I . . . was . . . scared . . . of . . . never . . . see . . . ing . . . a new leaf . . . again –'

The Buck Lep (*agitated*) For God's sake let's move! (*As they roll him on to the blanket soothingly.*) Ach now . . . easy.

THE BUCK LEP *opens the door carefully and peers into the street before they carry him out.*

SCENE 2

The factory. ROSALEEN *works at her bench.*

Newscaster – A Whitehall spokesman refused to comment. Following the discovery of the body of Mr Colm Doherty, father of four young children, in an alley way off Botanic Avenue, early this morning, the Royal Ulster Constabulary, warn people to check the credentials of drivers before hiring taxi-cabs.
During a gunbattle, in the Upper Falls Road, early today, in which an

estimated two hundred rounds were fired, an Army spokesman claimed two hits, possibly three –

The radio is drowned by a prolonged cheer. The music comes on.

JIM *enters slowly with his trolley and proceeds to load it up from her bench.*

Jim Did you hear that, fenian! Two hits, possibly three. Bet you know a thing or two about where you live. Well, come on, teague, tell us! Confirm it.
Rosaleen I'm . . . sorry . . . for you . . . Jim –

Startled, he drops a tray.

You have . . . forced our people . . . to die – Worse . . . gladly . . . die –

He watches with growing fear as she struggles, in a halting and stuttering way, to get the words out.

Can't stand . . . your taunts – No more! (*Banging the bench.*) Now . . . get the lift to Hell!

He backs away slowly before running.

Nuala (*approaching*) Did you hear them, Rosaleen?

She stands shyly looking at her.

Rosaleen Won't . . . bite you . . . Nuala.
Nuala Give me time to get used to you. (*Starting to go.*)
Rosaleen What time? No time . . . too much . . . to be done. The mother . . . must not . . . stand in . . . the way . . . of the child. The womb also held . . . the hand . . . that became the fist.

NUALA *looks at her a moment, walks a few yards, stops, turns round and looks at her again silently.*

Nuala Oh God, Rosaleen!

HELEN *approaches followed by* JIM. *They stand and stare at her a moment.*

Helen What are you doing up here, Quigley?

NUALA *starts to walk away.*

A minute of your time there!

NUALA *turns.*

(*To* JIM.) Get on with your work.

JIM *starts loading the trolley and slyly glances at them while trying to hear the conversation.*

You have not given me a proper explanation for your absence these last two days.

Nuala A close relative of mine was very ill.

Helen Do you have the same relative?

Rosaleen A neighbour . . . died.

Helen (*going closer to her*) Gunshot wounds?

Rosaleen (*stepping towards her*) Don't insult the stone . . . that talks. It's Father . . . might be . . . the mountain.

Helen Would there be a threat wrapped up in that?

Jim Ay, there is, Miss Shaw.

Helen (*turning angrily on him*) Get on with your work! So, you have decided to talk . . . after four years here.

She confronts ROSALEEN, *trying to outstare her.*

Nuala Rosaleen!

HELEN *abruptly exits, followed by* JIM *with his trolley.*

The lunch-time hooter blows.

Rosaleen (*as* NUALA *is about to go*) I'll . . . get it.

Nuala Get my sandwiches out of the solderin' room.

ROSALEEN *goes.* NUALA *leans on the bench in a depressed mood.*

Jim (*approaching cautiously*) Your mate's goin' to get into trouble and she's goin' to pull you down with her.

She doesn't answer.

I'm tellin' you, girl! We all think you're a great sport. You're even liked here. We don't mind people that can take a joke. (*Angrily.*) You better tell 'her' to keep quiet.

Nuala Here she comes . . . tell her yourself.

JIM *exits as* ROSALEEN *enters with the tea. She watches him as he goes.*

Rosaleen What did . . . he –? No, don't . . . tell me.

Nuala What's to become of us, Rosaleen?

Rosaleen I . . . could stop . . . talkin' –

Nuala Don't do that.

Rosaleen My throat . . . my tongue . . . sore.

Nuala All our hearts are truly warmed to hear you speak again, Rosaleen.

Rosaleen If smoke . . . comes out . . . of . . . a chimney . . . does it mean . . . a cosy fire? Smell . . . the smoke . . . watch . . . the colley . . . fall. Some mother . . . burns . . . old shoes . . . to keep . . . her children . . . warm. Sniff . . . the winds . . . tearin' through . . . Belfast. Words . . . are not mined . . . anymore. They come . . . from . . . the footwear . . . that kicked in . . . an innocent face. (*Pause.*) How . . . can I . . . stop talkin' now. (*Banging the bench.*) Even . . . if the ash settles on the red rose.

Nuala We'll be labelled security risks!

Rosaleen New words. Are teagues . . . and fenians . . . no longer . . . any good.

Nuala I don't think I can stay any longer in this factory.

Rosaleen With . . . the Prods . . . we are . . . natural enemies – The rabbit . . . and the stoat. (*Angrily.*) The days are gone . . . when they can pull me out of a hat!

A loud explosion nearby.

Nuala (*clutching at her*) Oh, Rosaleen!

Rosaleen A hundred pounder. Inside a buildin'.

Nuala (*pleading*) Let's go home.

Helen (*running in agitated*) Jim, Jim! Where's Jim! (*She exits.*)

Jim (*rushing in*) You want to see the flames in the sky! It must be Jackson's paint factory. (*He runs out.*)

Rosaleen It'll . . . look suspicious . . . if we go now.

Nuala I don't care. (*Crying.*) I want to go home.

Rosaleen Did . . . we make it?

Nuala NO!

Rosaleen Did . . . we plant it?

Nuala NO!

Rosaleen But . . . we wished it . . . deep down.

Nuala (*crying*) That's what I can't bear.

Rosaleen We can do . . . nothing . . . about that.

Putting on her coat.

Let's go . . . for the moment.

SCENE 3

Chanting (*before the lights come up*)
'Hail Mary! full of grace,
The Lord is with thee.
Blessed art thou among women.
And blessed is the fruit of thy womb, Jesus.
Holy Mary! Mother of God,
Pray for us sinners, now,
And at the hour of our death.
Amen.'

The prayer is repeated, over and over again during the following slide projection which shows the following notices from the death column of a newspaper.

QUINN: AUGUST 22 (KILLED IN ACTION)
LIAM, DEARLY BELOVED SON OF SADIE,
AND THE LATE OLIVER QUINN. RIP.
HIS REMAINS WILL BE MOVED TODAY

FOR THREE O'CLOCK REQUIEM MASS.
INTERNMENT IMMEDIATELY AFTERWARDS
IN MILLTOWN CEMETERY.
ON HIS SOUL SWEET JESUS HAVE MERCY.
DEEPLY REGRETTED BY HIS SORROWING MOTHER,
BROTHERS AND SISTERS AND FAMILY CIRCLE.

QUINN: AUGUST 22 (RESULT OF GUNSHOT WOUNDS)
THE NEIGHBOURS OF ROSE STREET
REGRET THE DEATH OF LIAM,
SON OF SADIE AND THE LATE OLIVER QUINN. RIP.
AND TENDER THEIR DEEPEST SYMPATHIES.
MOTHER OF PERPETUAL SUCCOUR, PRAY FOR HIM.
MASSES OFFERED.

QUINN: AUGUST 22 (KILLED IN ACTION)
THE POLITICAL REMAND PRISONERS, COMPOUND 2J,
LONG KESH CONCENTRATION CAMP,
EXPRESS DEEPEST SYMPATHY TO THE QUINN FAMILY.
WHERE PHILOSOPHIES MAY DIVIDE,
COURAGE WILL CONQUER, LIAM.

QUINN: AUGUST 22 (KILLED IN ACTION)
THE THIRD MACHINE-GUN UNIT
OF THE SECOND BATTALION OF VOLUNTEERS
REGRET TO ANNOUNCE THE DEATH OF THEIR
DEAR COMRADE VOLUNTEER LIAM QUINN
AND TENDER TO HIS BEREAVED MOTHER
AND FAMILY OUR AGONY AND HEART-FELT SYMPATHY.
HE THAT DIES FOR IRELAND: LIVES!

QUINN: AUGUST 22 (KILLED IN ACTION)
VOLUNTEER LIAM. IRELAND DIVIDED SHALL
NEVER BE FREE. DEEPLY REGRETTED
BY HIS SORROWING UNCLE DESSIE, AUNT AINE
AND COUSINS, ANDERSONSTOWN.
BE CLOSE TO HIM, LITTLE FLOWER.

QUINN: AUGUST 22 (RESULT OF GUNSHOT WOUNDS)
WEE LIAM, SHY LAMB IN THE CITY OF THE HOPELESS.
YOUR OWN TERESA.
ALSO FROM MARIE ON LOOM SIX,
BLACK MOUNTAIN SPINNING MILL.

Lights up.

'The Searched House'. A low light burns. Liam lies in his coffin, the lid of which leans upright against a wall. Flowers and Mass Cards cover the body to the neck.

A Hooded Figure, wearing a black beret and combat jacket, stands to attention near the coffin, holding a sub-machine gun.

SADIE, *wearing a black beret, enters holding a lighted candelabrum, followed by* THE BUCK LEP. ROSALEEN, MATILDA *and* NUALA *enter next wearing Mass mantillas. They all wear black arm bands and carry black flags.*

They stand a moment chanting 'The Hail Mary' and continue as each character approaches the coffin.

Matilda (*crossing herself*) Dear God, no more! Let this be the last. This boy could die, and in dyin', the world will whirl no faster now as it carries his unfilled brain and frame in a dark recess on its back. Who will reach him now but the blinded worm . . . to feed off his two-page epitaph to Life. Yet, along came a singer singin' a tone-deaf song and hittin' his tunein' fork upon a rock started this convulsion . . . and we sat back and applauded as the deadly notes rose from the music sheet and struck him down.

Rosaleen (*shouting*) Peace . . . can not be invented!

MATILDA *crosses herself, steps back and takes part in the chanting.*

The Buck Lep (*glancing at* ROSALEEN *as he approaches the coffin*) Let's have a bit of respect for the dead. (*Crossing himself and thinking a moment.*) I want peace as well . . . like Matilda. But we never knew peace. What would it be like? And if we get it . . . what do we do with it? And what do we do with all those things:
The muscles built for war.
The songs invented in the cause of it.
The insults stuck in our brains like broken glass.
The trust that the Protestants never gave us.
The graves at Milltown.
The tales of the dead Irish warriours lyin'
printed in the bookshops.
What do we do?
(*With sudden horror.*) If I can't keep the peace, I must keep the war in as safe a way as I know.

He crosses himself and joins in the chanting.

Rosaleen (*beside the coffin, crossing herself*) See, mother . . . I was silent . . . but you are blind. You taught me . . . agony . . . when it was just Life. Tears . . . meant misery . . . when they were . . . Spring showers . . . for the eyes. I . . . was the 'stone' . . . from the Diamond district. (*Fiercely.*) I

... am born again. I ... have bloomed. (*She bows to the coffin, crosses herself and joins in the chanting.*)

They look at NUALA *as she hesitates before approaching the coffin.*

Nuala (*in agony*) Please, God, tell me what has happened!

MATILDA *leads her away. The chanting stops.*

Matilda What can I say to youse all. What can I even say to my only daughter Rosaleen. What can I say as a mother who has only seen the very sun, in the sky, as the hob-nailed sole of a boot ... who can only guess at Life. 'Nervous is the beaten cur who misses a day without the stick.' We are free ... Yes ... FREE. 'Love thy neighbour as thyself. Forgive them for they know not what they have done.' Say anything ... take out the hoary old words again. Use them till we find something better. Guess Life ... guess Death.

SADIE *approaches* MATILDA *and looks fiercely at her. She raises her hand to strike her but decides against it.*

Sadie (*beside the coffin, furiously crossing herself with her clenched fist, harshly*) Will you listen to them, son! My boy, my boy, my wee boy, mammy's baby, listen to them. Tell them what has happened. Don't they know there has been an uprisin'! Do we have to tar it upon every brick in every wall on every rock on every stone that makes up this heap beneath our feet. (*Shouting.*) Somebody was keepin' us down! And those who were our masters went back to rule in the same old way. But, we will continue fightin' ... because an elephant cannot be sandpapered down to a grey-hound. We will cover the streets with our wet-nursin' weans to stop the saracens. I am not like some who talk about the mercy of the world while we're bein' sledge-hammered to death in our own back yards. (*Turning to the coffin.*) God love you, Liam. It's a great pity you didn't have another life to give. (*Kissing him on the lips.*) I'll be with you, son, when duty's done. (*To the hooded figure.*) Nail down the lid before he hears anymore of their spineless talk!

THE HOODED FIGURE *lifts the coffin lid.* MATILDA *and* NUALA *shrink back as he approaches the coffin.* THE BUCK LEP *takes one end of the lid. They screw it down.*

SADIE *walks to the head of the coffin with the short, heavy beat-step of the Republican Movement.*

She jumps to attention and salutes. THE HOODED FIGURE *beat-steps, jumps to attention and salutes.*

ROSALEEN *hesitates before slowly bringing her hand up to salute.*

The record: 'I'm Free' sung by Roger Daltrey (from the ODE album 'Tommy', ODE 99001).

SCENE 4

The MCGURK'*s home.* ROSALEEN *sits reading a book.* MATILDA *sews.*

THE BUCK LEP *bursts through the door in a crouching position.*

The Buck Lep Get on the floor quick! There's goin' to be trouble.

They throw themselves flat on the floor.

They've commandeered my house. I sent Philomena and the kids to my mother's.

Rosaleen This is for . . . wee Liam.

Automatic fire breaks out.

The Buck Lep Keep your heads down!
Rosaleen That's all . . . we have ever done.
The Buck Lep The Army will search my house after they have gone.
Rosaleen But Liam . . . died.
The Buck Lep What a bloody mess that'll be!
Matilda If they stop now they'll be in time for the 'Nine O'clock News' –
Rosaleen Keep quiet. Think of . . . Liam.
Matilda Is this a memorial service?
Rosaleen Mother!
Matilda I'll remember him in my own way.
The Buck Lep I can't hear the shootin' for the talkin'.

The gunfire starts to peter out except for occasional shots.

Rosaleen Don't move! It's 'A' Company.
Matilda Hmmmph! That's some consolation.
Rosaleen They've got a different pattern to . . . their fire.
Matilda Promote that girl on the floor to General.
Rosaleen Wait . . . till you hear.

Two long bursts of automatic fire.

Told you!
The Buck Lep Keep down!
Rosaleen They . . . should be withdrawin' now.
Matilda Hope they don't come through here.
The Buck Lep Probably 'Oilcloth Avenue'.
Rosaleen Never! Don't you know . . . your underground . . . escape routes!
Matilda Turn the Sacred Heart lamp to green, there's traffic waitin'.

The firing dies away. An armoured car roars into the street.

They stand up.

The Buck Lep They've come for the spring-sewin' – diggin' in the sofa with picks and shovels, hoein' behind the Devon-grate . . . ploughin' the plaster – No wonder the man said: 'In a nation on the run only the portable arts survive.'

Rosaleen Sure, you can't even draw, Buck Lep.

Matilda It's no joke, Rosaleen.

The Buck Lep Sideboards and saracens, red-glass swans and Royal Marine Commandos.

A heavy bang on the door before it is flung open. The SOLDIER, *his face blacked-out, stands in the doorway.*

Soldier (*pointing at* THE BUCK LEP) You don't live here.

Rosaleen Neither do you.

Soldier I remember you! You work in that electronic's factory.

Rosaleen And I remember you too, Brit.

Soldier Sussed me out, eh.

Rosaleen You're stupid. (*Indicating* MATILDA *and* THE BUCK LEP.) Why do you terrorise . . . innocent people.

Soldier And you . . . innocent?

Rosaleen Goin' to arrest me?

Soldier It would be a pleasure, love.

Rosaleen Keep that talk for your whore.

The Buck Lep For Christ's sake stop it, both of you!

He takes out a packet of cigarettes and offers one to the SOLDIER.

Here.

As the SOLDIER *reaches for it* ROSALEEN *knocks it from his hand and crushes it underfoot.*

Soldier (*to* THE BUCK LEP) Silly bastard! Stay here – all of you – till we check everybody out. (*He exits.*)

Matilda In the name of God, Rosaleen!

Rosaleen (*looking at him a moment*) So, that's what . . . you call . . . 'keepin' the war'.

Sadie (*entering quickly*) The 'lads' must have given it to them! Saw a saracen ambulance racin' mad along Albert Street.

The Buck Lep Holy Jesus, they didn't have armoured ambulances during the last world war!

Sadie (*turning on him*) They seem to have finished with your house. Saw one big 'glyp' of a soldier comin' out with a pneumatic drill in his hand.

The Buck Lep Ah, Jesus Christ, drillin' for oil! That beats the lot.

Matilda Ach, Sadie, don't make it worse for him.

Sadie If I were you, Buck Lep, I'd buy a tent and pitch it in Falls Park.

The Buck Lep You tell your 'friends' they better pay for the damage to my house. (*He exits.*)

Matilda (*into the street*) That's the idea, Buck Lep. I'm with you!

Sadie Blamin' it on us. The Brits smashed my father's toilet bowl . . . remember. He sat on it in the dark and had to get seven stitches in the Mater Hospital.

Rosaleen Streets have ceased to be places . . . you shout into . . . around here, Mother.

Matilda You're startin' to worry me, Rosaleen.

Sadie Did I interrupt something.

Matilda A childhood? (*Pointing.*) A photograph on a wall? A soldier blackin' out his face? A sixteen-year-old ghost clutchin' a rifle on a roof top – ?

SADIE *adjusts her black arm band and smoothes it fondly.*

Sadie Yes, you were sayin'.

Matilda A widow threatened with the tribe? Maybe not a perfect man . . . but a man just the same . . . in the broken eggshell of his home? A friend who speaks buckets of blood? What mortal could interrupt this! What god could intervene either . . . even if He came here with the Pope and all his cardinals and made us a Venice with their holy water, and a foggy sea-coast with their incense, and raised the host ten thousand times to the blisterin' sky.

Sadie That's too grand for our neighbourhood, Matilda. We're more like whelks waitin' to be picked out of our shells.

Rosaleen You're wrong . . . Mother.

Matilda (*picking up a shovel and grabbing a broom*) I promised to help the Buck Lep. (*She exits.*)

Rosaleen She's . . . wrong . . . Mrs Quinn.

Sadie (*with a knowing nod*) Action speaks louder than words.

A knock on the door and NUALA *enters, dressed for travelling and carrying a suitcase.*

Nuala I thought I'd call before I go.

Rosaleen Where!

Nuala I'll never go back to the factory.

Rosaleen Sit down.

Nuala I haven't much time. I'm gettin' the Liverpool boat at Donegal Quay.

Rosaleen Why . . . didn't you tell me! Sit down a minute.

Nuala No.

Rosaleen Don't go.

Nuala I must.

Rosaleen I'll . . . leave you down.

Nuala No. I want to look at the place for the last time – store up as much as I can remember.

Rosaleen It's . . . final.

Nuala Final.

Sadie We need everybody!

Rosaleen Will . . . you be all right?

Nuala I'm goin' to my auntie's in Bolton.

Sadie We have a few contacts there.

Rosaleen Sounds . . . a long journey.

Nuala For the body, a short distance. For the mind, forever.

Rosaleen Well . . . all the best. (*They hug.*)

Sadie (*waving her hand casually as if dismissing her*) Maybe you'll come back married to us, Nuala.

NUALA *exits.*

Rosaleen (*into the street*) Thank you . . . for lookin' after me.

Sadie She could have become disaffected – dangerous.

ROSALEEN *breaks down sobbing.*

SCENE 5

The factory. A few minutes before lunch time. ROSALEEN *works, humming to herself.*

JIM *approaches pulling his trolley and singing.*

Jim   'Hitler has only got one ball.
       Goering has two but they are small.
       Himmler is something similar,
       But poor oul' Goebbels has no balls at all –'

Rosaleen (*pointing her nose in the air*) We – I don't want to hear . . . anymore.

Jim My oul' lad was celebratin' the war again last night. My oul' doll came into the kitchen and opened up the second front. (*He imitates the sound of a bugle.*) The battle moved to the scullery then back to the kitchen. (*Jumping around with an imaginary gun in his hand.*) He captured the fireside chair, after fierce hand-to-hand fightin', but he lost it again when she re-attacked on a suicide mission. The television on 'Hill Six' fell next. He retreated with his battered battalions to the pigeon house – You should have seen the feathers as he sent up a couple of regiments to search the arse-hole of the night for the 'Kamikaze'.

Rosaleen (*tutting*) Youse seem to live a rip-roarin' life.

Jim There's many's a good tale comes out of a good bottle of protestant whiskey.

Rosaleen Youse are almost . . . human.

Jim You watch yourself now, girl.

He grabs her, making her squeal.

Helen (*approaching quickly*) Get about your work this minute, Sloane!

Jim (*singing as he exits*)
         'It's a long way up the Shankill.
         It's a long way to go.
         It's a long way up the Shankill.

To the only girl I know.
Goodbye Piccadilly, goodbye Leicester Square.
It's a long, long way up the Shankill,
For my heart lies there.'

Helen (*watching him with a scowl on her face*) I'll get him one of these days.

The hooter blows. As ROSALEEN *is about to exit,* JIM *approaches with two cups of tea carefully balanced on his trolley. He puts one on her bench and then sits on his trolley some distance away.*

Jim (*regretfully*) Your mate's gone. She's missed.

Rosaleen (*standing up*) Oh God . . . I should have stayed a 'stone'.

Jim (*choking on his tea*) What?

Rosaleen I was doubtful all along . . . Jim. You . . . don't know. None of us know . . . what we are doin'.

Jim (*laughing*) Will I get Nurse Gillespie? She has tranquillisers –

Rosaleen (*smiling*) What can cure a turn for the better?

Jim Would you like to sit here?

Rosaleen Is it an honour . . . to sit on your trolley?

Jim Ay, it is.

He moves his trolley closer.

Rosaleen (*sitting down*) Cosy . . . despite.

Jim We Prods and Cats are different.

Rosaleen That's awful true.

Jim We even use different guns.

Rosaleen (*slapping him on the back*) God . . . you're an awful 'gaunch'! But it's nice to be friends.

Jim Like when my oul' lad says: 'Commere, you watery lookin' being you, till I break an arm or two!' I know he's in a good mood. But when he says: 'Jim', like his tongue has been cooked, I always duck quick and cover my face. You would understand that? Wouldn't you?

Rosaleen Up my way when they say: 'That's a fine boy . . . a good-hearted lad.' He's usually half-way down . . . the hole with the slanty sides.

Jim Sad, isn't it.

Rosaleen Terrible.

Jim Ay, it is.

Rosaleen Yet, Jim . . . I'll have to go through with it.

Jim So will I, Rosaleen.

Rosaleen Still . . . it's better than moralisin'.

Jim (*thinking*) What does that word mean?

Rosaleen 'Belongin' to manners and conduct . . . guided by the moral law'?

He shakes his head.

Makes no sense to me either – Out of date belchin' by out-of-date leaders, tryin' to hold their jobs and keep the old ways?

Jim Moralisin' – must remember that.
Rosaleen They leave us to pull up the weeds, then, they'll boot us out . . . and plant flowers.
Jim Who's 'they'?
Rosaleen Don't know yet.
Jim Tell us when you find out.
Rosaleen I'll . . . do that.

> *They sit a moment in silence.*

Jim 'They' better not be protestants.
Rosaleen Or catholics!
Jim Ay, all right then.
Rosaleen (*putting out her hand*) Shake.

> *He shakes her hand and attempts to kiss her.*

> (*Drawing away.*) Don't mix business with pleasure.

> HELEN *approaches slowly, wiping her eyes. She stands still until* JIM *catches sight of her.*

Jim (*jumping up*) Is it a strike? I didn't hear any bombs go off.

> HELEN *uncovers her eyes, drops her hands and cries softly.* JIM *rushes to her and holds her. She whispers.*

> ROSALEEN *grimly gets up and goes behind her bench.*

Jim Rosaleen, oh God, Rosaleen, her boyfriend has been killed by a sniper!
Helen In your area. (*Screaming.*) Kill her!

> ROSALEEN *picks up a hammer as* JIM *approaches.*

Jim Go quick, Rosaleen!
Rosaleen (*raising the hammer*) It wasn't me.
Helen One of you did!
Jim Please, Rosaleen.
Rosaleen (*banging the hammer on the bench*) NO!

> HELEN *rushes off crying loudly.*

Jim You better!
Helen's Voice Get that fenian bitch out of here.
Jim (*panic stricken*) Hear that! She's stirrin' it up.
Rosaleen I stay.

> *Suddenly, hammers start beating benches in a rhythm.*

Jim (*twirling his chain with the bullet*) That's only the start. (*Looking up the factory.*) The other teagues are goin'. (*Shouting.*) Get your coat on!
Rosaleen (*crossing herself*) Fuck off!

She raises the hammer.

JIM *backs away.*

Voices (*singing, accompanied by hammer beats*)
      'Fight, fight, fight for Ulster.
      Fight for our dearest Land.
      We have got a bloody gun,
      And we'll make you quickly run.
      Like the Kaiser-man and all his fuckin' huns.'
Jim (*listening*) The oul' blood is racin'. There's time yet. (*Shouting.*) Leave!

She casually shakes her head and smiles faintly.

Voice The popehead whore must go!
Jim If I'm seen talkin' to you much longer they'll think I'm a teague-lover.
(*Glancing up the factory.*) Get out!

She smashes the hammer down on the bench.

JIM *exits.*

Silence falls as she arranges spanners, a milk bottle and pieces of metal into a pile on the bench.

Someone throws a half-brick. She picks it up, puts it on the bench and picks up the hammer.

A drum starts beating. JIM *marches in followed by* HELEN *who carries a Red Hand flag of Ulster.*

JIM *mounts the trolley and reads awkwardly from a piece of paper.*

Jim 'Since all reasonable approaches have been turned down by the teague Rosaleen McGurk, I, Jim Sloane, leader of the Shower of Hail and its associated bodies, hereby show the flag and re-dedicate this factory to protestantism and Ulster. We warn her that she cannot remain within the precincts of this memorial to our faith and province.

A drum beats as they march around.

Rosaleen Jim.

Startled, he looks at her.

    That's not you.
Jim 'Tis.
Helen You have broken your oath of silence to the teague.

The drum beats on for a time before there is silence.

She dodges as a hail of missiles hits her bench. She throws the spanners up the factory in reply.

A missile hits her and she falls stunned. A cheer goes up.

JIM *rushes forward to pick her up but is felled himself. He scrambles to his feet and drags* ROSALEEN *away.*

HELEN *rushes forward weeping and plants the flag on* ROSALEEN's *bench.*

(*Screaming.*) Don't come back, Sloane!

A loud cheer goes up and voices start singing:

Voices   'Fight, fight, fight for Ulster, etc.'

SCENE 6

The MCGURK's *home . . . about three p.m.*

MATILDA *tends to* ROSALEEN *and* JIM, *washing the blood off their heads and faces.*

Rosaleen He's mad comin' up here.
Matilda Don't think about if for a moment.
Jim We saw this bus and just hopped it.
Rosaleen I told you . . . I'd be all right.
Jim I was dazed. How did I know I'd end up the Falls!
Rosaleen Jim . . . you don't know what you have done.
Matilda Try and rest. (*To* JIM.) I'll think of some way of gettin' you out safe.

JIM *gets up and walks around the room looking at the religious emblems and the black-draped photograph.*

Haven't you been in a catholic house before?
Jim Never in my life. (*Pointing at the Sacred Heart lamp.*) What's that?
Matilda That's a Sacred Heart lamp.
Jim What do youse use it for?
Rosaleen Stop askin' so many questions!
Matilda Have some manners, Rosaleen.
Jim (*pointing at the photograph*) Who's that?
Rosaleen That's my daddy.
Jim Is he dead or something?
Rosaleen He died for his country.
Matilda (*sternly*) Now, that's enough, Rosaleen.
Jim We usually only have a bible in our house and a knocker on the door showin' King William on his horse.
Rosaleen (*making a face*) God, that's weird!
Matilda What else, son –

A knock on the door before someone tries to open it. They freeze for a moment. MATILDA *hurriedly leads* JIM *into a back room. She returns and unlocks the door.* SADIE *enters.*

Sadie (*looking closely at the lock*) Something wrong with your door?

Matilda God, I'm away in the head today! Must have locked it without thinkin'.

Sadie You're home early today, Rosaleen. (*Looking closer at her.*) What's wrong with YOU?

Matilda She had an accident at work.

Sadie (*looking suspiciously around*) Do you get the feelin' that there's somebody else in this house?

Matilda I feel like that when I'm alone sometimes. (*Looking at the photo.*) But it's always complete imagination.

Sadie One of your neighbour's boys reckon they saw a stranger around here.

Matilda Ach, you know what children are like . . . especially these days.

Sadie This was a young lad wearin' blue denims.

Matilda Young Joey up the street wears them.

Sadie They said he looked protestant – sort of flat-faced and transparent lookin'.

Matilda A protestant would be an utter insane case to come up here.

Sadie That's what I said. But the occasional one does. You know what they're like for dope and drink – maybe got a wrong bus under the influence.

Matilda Then no harm would be done.

Sadie I said that as well, but, the risk couldn't be taken. They could very well take back a list of victims for their execution squads.

Matilda Thanks for tryin' to protect us, Sadie.

Sadie It's only our duty to the Street Defence Committee.

Rosaleen But . . . this is not your street, Mrs Quinn.

Sadie Ay, true, but this could be a job for the Central Council. (*Staring at her.*) What kind of an accident did you have?

Rosaleen Slipped . . . oil on the factory floor . . . hit my head on a girder.

Sadie Will you be goin' back to work shortly?

Rosaleen If I want to . . . mightn't though.

Sadie You wouldn't give up a good job, with good pay, just like that.

Rosaleen You have no right to question –

Matilda (*laughing*) Ach, you sound like a policeman, Sadie.

Sadie Yes, that's true, but, guess who for. (*To* ROSALEEN.) You were sayin'.

Rosaleen It's a bit lonely there . . . without Nuala.

Sadie When did you decide that?

Rosaleen I'll feel the way I want . . . and decide what I want.

Sadie Not these days. We've got to know what people are up to. The security of the area depends on it.

Matilda You can depend on our judgement, Sadie.

Sadie (*cynically*) Yes. (*To* ROSALEEN.) There's been a lot of trouble at your factory.

Rosaleen A bit.

Sadie A bit! (*Taking a notebook out of her pocket and turning the pages.*) Know anything about a certain five-man committee rulin' there?

Matilda Let her rest, Sadie, she's not feelin' too well.

Sadie We want them . . . badly.

Matilda (*firmly gripping the back of a chair*) Search the bloody place!

Sadie (*ignoring her*) What about the other Catholics workin' there?

Rosaleen Oh, they're from the Short Strand.

Sadie (*looking at her notebook*) What's their names?

Rosaleen Florrie . . . I think . . . Padraic – And the old woman Anastasia.

Sadie Their surnames and exact addresses?

Matilda Have a bit of sense. Who's goin' to reveal they're from the Short Strand –

Rosaleen Catholics or not.

Sadie That's only a short ride across town. We'll check up. (*She puts her notebook in her pocket.*)

Matilda Well, that's that. Now, how about a nice cup of tea?

Sadie No thanks. I've got some urgent work to do. See you again.

She exits. MATILDA *goes to lock the door.*

Rosaleen (*alarmed*) Don't!

They stay silent until SADIE *re-appears.*

Sadie There's a quare sale goin' on at Robinson Cleavers. The bed-sheets are real cheap. So long again. (*She exits.*)

Matilda Need I say she's suspicious.

Rosaleen We'll have to get him out of here . . . quick!

They keep quiet for some time before MATILDA *locks the door and brings* JIM *into the room.*

Jim Who was that?

Matilda We don't know that person.

Rosaleen (*to* JIM) Heard anything?

Matilda (*quickly*) You couldn't hear very much.

Jim I'm in trouble as well – (*Panic stricken.*) I'm dead!

Rosaleen We'll get you out safely –

Jim If – You don't know what they're like in my area. I'll get a hidin' when I get back. A four-day-in-the-hospital-beatin'. They have it all worked out like surgeons! (*Bitterly, to* ROSALEEN.) For helpin' you.

Matilda Come here, son. (*Hugging.*) You're a young man and will mend quickly.

Rosaleen Maybe if we explain to Sadie –

Matilda No names!

Rosaleen Hysteria.

Matilda Hysteria.

Rosaleen (*shaking her head regretfully*) There's too much of it about at the moment.

Matilda I wonder if – You know our neighbour, Rosaleen? Would that body be about repairin' a house? Don't open that door till you hear three knocks.

She exits. ROSALEEN *bolts the door.*

Rosaleen That's the end of the factory.
Jim I'll miss my trolley.
Rosaleen Nothing else?
Jim Not a thing.
Rosaleen (*disappointed*) Are you sure?
Jim (*irritably*) Certain.
Rosaleen No more to be said . . . to each other.
Jim When I came into this world they didn't open the frilly curtains to let me through.
Rosaleen (*teasing*) Ah, Jim, did they not.
Jim A man's got to be tough. He's got to weld on his boots and dip his fists into the brine.
Rosaleen His heart as well?
Jim That needs special treatment – stainless-steel rivets to keep it in place.

ROSALEEN *tuts and shakes her head teasingly.*

Mention the moon when you're at it.
Rosaleen What about the moon, Jim?
Jim It's a big manhole cover that needs liftin'.
Rosaleen The wee stars? The twinkly wee stars?
Jim Bungholes for waste water.
Rosaleen (*teasing*) Ah, that's a shame. (*Quickly.*) Spring?
Jim My woolly vest starts to itch.
Rosaleen That's what I call a truthful factory hand's view of the world.
Jim Hold on there, girl, I like to smell flowers.
Rosaleen It's too late. You're hopeless, Jim.

JIM *looks disappointed. She gently puts her hand on his face.*

Three knocks on the door. She opens it cautiously. MATILDA *enters followed by* THE BUCK LEP, *carrying a bricklayer's trowel. He circles the room, looking suspiciously at* JIM.

This is –
The Buck Lep (*waving the trowel*) No names! This is goin' to take a bit of thinkin' out.
Matilda There's little time left.
The Buck Lep That Mrs 'Thingummybob' is as sharp as a bottle in the 'Docker's Arms'.
Rosaleen Your friend's car?
The Buck Lep Sharin' a big secret makes it no smaller.
Matilda A black taxi?

The Buck Lep Why don't you shout it from the top of Cavehill.

Rosaleen Would he pass . . . for one of us?

The Buck Lep (*looking at him a moment*) Boy, you may as well have come up here wearin' an orange sash. Look at him!

They look at him a moment.

Jim (*uncomfortably*) What's wrong with me?

The Buck Lep Fella, you're not only a protestant, but you have the misfortune of lookin' like one.

Matilda Ach now!

The Buck Lep No offence meant, oul' hand, but it's like tryin' to pass off haddock as hare around here.

Rosaleen Disguise him.

The Buck Lep That's an idea!

Rosaleen Put a priest's collar on him.

The Buck Lep It's the priests that have to disguise themselves today in case they're taken for gunmen on the run.

Rosaleen A nun?

The Buck Lep That's reserved for commanders.

Matilda Hey, are you on your 'geg' or something!

The Buck Lep (*to* JIM) It is a joke. (*To* MATILDA.) Then again –

Rosaleen (*teasing*) I'll lend him one of my dresses.

The Buck Lep The very thing!

Jim What are youse talkin' about?

The Buck Lep (*inscribing the air with his trowel*) Here's the picture: Rosaleen's third cousin has come to visit her a few hours before goin' back to her job as nanny to the Simpson-Jameson family on the Malone Road – Is it rich-to-sickenin' enough! Somebody's become a 'Late' in her family. She's been to Mass and still wears her mantilla with a death-band on her arm. Nobody looks twice at mourners today – For Christ's sake the whole city is mournin'!

Matilda (*going to the door and listening*) Hurry.

The Buck Lep (*to* JIM) Let's have a look at you. You need a shave. (*To* MATILDA.) Got a razor?

Matilda Where's the men in this house!

The Buck Lep Your legs?

Matilda Sandpaper.

Rosaleen Cream.

The Buck Lep Jesus, that's desperate! Just like a bloody woman to be awkward. (*He starts to go.*)

Matilda Three knocks mind you! (*He exits.*)

Rosaleen (*to* JIM) God, you're goin' to be lovely!

Jim Can't I just make a dash for it?

Matilda The whole district's full of oul' women stitchin' hoods.

Rosaleen What's it goin' to be?

Jim Miss Sloane, I presume.

Rosaleen Walk like a woman. (*She turns on the radio for music.*) Watch me. (*She walks slowly around the room.*) No, no, that's an eight-pint Guinness walk. Like this. (*She walks around the room again and stops very close to him.*) You've got to have a slight swivel . . . from the hips.

Jim I don't have those joints.

Rosaleen Pretend them. (*She walks again.*)

Jim This is hopeless.

Rosaleen Again!

They walk again.

Three knocks on the door. ROSALEEN *switches off the radio.* MATILDA *cautiously opens it.*

The Buck Lep Go and have a shave quick.

MATILDA *points.* JIM *takes the brush, soap and razor and exits.*

(*Hushed tones.*) There's a Volunteer patrol out.

Matilda Are the buses runnin'?

The Buck Lep If there's no trouble, there'll be no hi-jackin'.

Rosaleen I'll go and sort some clothes out. (*She exits.*)

Matilda He doesn't appear a bad lad – I mean, not a deliberate one.

The Buck Lep The 'Big Bugs' started this war. Now let them get out of it themselves.

Matilda Fox-huntin' rats on horseback!

The Buck Lep Come rain, hail, or shite they'll survive . . . and us – we'll have to rebuild the ruins . . . those of us left survivin'.

Matilda For God's sake survive, Buck Lep!

The Buck Lep Yourself as well, Matilda.

Rosaleen (*entering and holding up a pair of shoes*) Will these do?

The Buck Lep (*looking closely at them*) Them's for feet as slippery as an eel's.

Rosaleen Like practical women, eh, Buck Lep, with jail warder's shoes on.

The Buck Lep Go on give my head peace, and get him into some clothes.

She exits.

MATILDA *kneels before the Sacred Heart lamp praying.*

Matilda (*crossing herself and rising*) Just in case it comes in handy.

The Buck Lep No need to apologise to me, Matilda. Keep the lines open to Divil, Man, God and Irish red-setter.

Matilda Had a wild dream the other night – Or, was it because I turned badly in my sleep? Cricked my neck and an ear rang. 'God, I've been shot! Is this how it will feel?'

The Buck Lep We're saturated. The brain's bubblin' over with ill-feelin', it's runnin' out of the gills of our arse.

Matilda (*knocking on the door*) Hurry up!

Rosaleen's Voice Just a minute. (*She starts giggling before breaking into a loud laugh.*)

Matilda Keep your voice down. 'Her' next door'll think we're runnin' a bad house.

The Buck Lep (*to himself*) Morality at a time like this? Some people can't be cured.

Rosaleen (*giggling*) Are youse ready? Here we come.

The door opens and JIM *appears, supported by* ROSALEEN, *wearing a dress, cardigan and necklace and wobbling on* ROSALEEN'*s shoes.*

Matilda (*putting her hand over her mouth*) God, it doesn't seem natural!

Rosaleen (*trying not to giggle*) But we live in dangerous times.

The Buck Lep Holy Jesus, I had a sister in the marines who looked better.

Jim Give us a chance for God's sake!

Rosaleen (*walking him around the room*) Doesn't your feet bend!

Jim The whole bloody place is bent.

Rosaleen Sit down for make-up.

The Buck Lep Give him the sunken eyes of the teague.

Rosaleen (*starting to make him up*) I'm not so sure if I like that, Buck –

The Buck Lep (*alarmed*) No names now!

Rosaleen A bit here . . . a bit there – Stay still till I get the lashes on.

Matilda (*arranging the mantilla on his head*) That was my sister's. 'How's it over there?' she asks from Birmingham. 'It's sad, very sad', I answer. (*Fixing on the black arm band.*) Even a golden pen writes rust these days.

Rosaleen Now, there we are!

Jim (*standing up and patting his chin*) Is the shave close enough? I can't bear to look in the mirror.

The Buck Lep (*looking closely*) That's as close as we might ever get.

Matilda Hope you have seen us. Like, we're just ordinary people.

Jim So are we, misses. I'll try and remember.

The Buck Lep We'll still be the same, fella.

Rosaleen You won't remember, Jim. (*Putting her hand over her mouth.*) God, I might forget, too!

The Buck Lep (*to* JIM) You're Mary O'Neil, if we're stopped.

Matilda (*peeping into the street*) It looks clear but I can't see properly.

The Buck Lep Let's rummage the streets for the all-clear. You take the back street and I'll take the one to the bus stop.

Matilda (*impatient*) Come on!

They exit. ROSALEEN *bolts the door. They wait in silence, listening.*

Jim Will I ever see you again, Rosaleen?

Rosaleen (*brightening*) Well, ah –

Jim We could meet in the city centre.

Rosaleen NO!

Jim At the 'Candlelight'?

Rosaleen What good would that be!

Jim Try. (*He takes her hand.*)

Rosaleen I . . . couldn't go to your area. You couldn't come to mine. We wouldn't know each other. You've got . . . to understand each other's way of life. Like the parents meetin' –

Jim What! (*He puts his arm around her but she shakes it off.*)

Rosaleen – And all the brothers and sisters . . . the aunties, the uncles. That could be war enough –

Jim No, it wouldn't –

Rosaleen – And the grandmas . . . and the grandpas sayin' 'there's a teague in the family blood! . . . there's a prod in our sacred heritage!' No.

Jim Please. (*He puts his arm around her again. She shakes it off more slowly.*)

Rosaleen I'll probably end up marryin' . . . a bullet-scarred, unskilled labourer . . . with a nun-sister in Dar es Salaam. (*Walking away quickly.*) Besides, the war's not over. I don't know what I'll think when you leave this house. I'll probably hate you tomorrow . . . and shoot you . . . if you ever invade our area. (*She turns her back on him.*)

Jim (*pacing the room with his hands tightly together*) I'll marry a mill girl – a 'greasy belly'. God's curse on her if she marries a skilled man first!

Rosaleen (*involuntarily*) No! (*He goes towards her.*) Yes.

Jim (*stopping*) Yes. I'll look for a wee house, just like the one in my mother's street – so as we can feel safe. I'll build a pigeon loft, go to the pub, swop tales about the teagues – (*Going towards her.*) For God's sake, Rosaleen! (*To himself.*) Help me. (*Stamping hard on the floor.*) I'll learn my children to hate the teagues. (*Looking at her.*) What else is there to do! I'd be moralisin' if I didn't.

They look at each other helplessly in a moment of silence.

But I'll still look and look till I see the roofs of the Falls. For beneath one of them grey lids there's a girl called Rosaleen McGurk or maybe Rosaleen 'Somethingelse' by then.

Rosaleen (*softly, almost a whisper*) Jim! (*He goes to her.*) No, don't come near me. I'll look too, up the night-avenue of 'The Hammer' and imagine you there . . . behind a draughty window. I'll . . . be fat, carryin' a shoppin' bag of frozen foods, steadyin' the last child on its walkin' reins . . . worryin'. You'll . . . have a vein-broken face from drinkin' – I want to see no more. (*Gritting her teeth.*) There's a boy . . . with a trolley . . . called Jim Sloane.

Jim Let me kiss you, Rosaleen.

Rosaleen (*walking away from him*) Why not . . . another memory.

He follows her. For a moment she stiffens but relaxes as he kisses her.

Rosaleen You're supposed to say: 'mind my hair, watch my make-up.'

They hold each other until there are three knocks on the door. THE BUCK LEP *dashes in followed by* MATILDA.

The Buck Lep A Volunteer patrol are havin' whiskey-tea in a house up the street.

MATILDA opens the door of the back room and pulls out a brown paper parcel.

Matilda Don't forget to take your clothes, son.

The Buck Lep You stay here, Rosaleen. (*To* JIM.) We'll go with you in a bus to the city centre. Ready? (*He peeps into the street.*) Now!

Jim (*taking the bullet and chain off*) Don't be offended.

He places it around ROSALEEN's *neck.*

That's all I've got.

The Buck Lep (*looking at the chain*) What! Christ, come double quick!

Rosaleen (*patting* JIM's *face with a powder-puff*) There!

The Buck Lep There's a bus due.

Matilda Will you be all right?

ROSALEEN nods.

The Buck Lep (*grabbing the parcel*) Now, for fuck's sake!

Before they exit MATILDA *looks at* ROSALEEN *in a questioning sort of way. She rushes to the door, kisses* MATILDA *and then crosses herself.*

ROSALEEN *fondles the chain and puts the bullet out of sight beneath the neck of her dress. She quickly tidies up the room, puts the radio on, and whilst listening to the pop music, wanders restlessly around the room.*

She stops before the black-draped photograph of her father a moment. She switches off the radio and sits down quietly.

There is a heavy knock on the door and SADIE *enters.*

Sadie All alone, Rosaleen?

Rosaleen Completely.

Sadie Mind if I look in that room?

Rosaleen You'll be wastin' your time.

SADIE *rushes into the room.*

Sadie's Voice Oh my God! (*Entering.*) That heavy, sludgy, twisty-ankled, boyish-lookin' girl – He's escaped! (*She rushes to the door.*)

Rosaleen One moment! Let me give you a vital tool for workin' out the finer details of your 'Golden Age'.

She exits and returns holding LIAM's *sub-machinegun in a firing position.*

Sadie (*backing away*) The place is hivin' with Volunteers.

Rosaleen (*throwing it on the floor*) Take wee Liam's gun and go.

SADIE *hesitates.*

(*Pulling her to the gun.*) Pick it up!

SADIE *picks up the gun and backs out of the room into the street.*

ROSALEEN *bolts the door and piles some furniture against it.*

Sadie's Voice (*shouting*) Call Dessie . . . they have helped the spy to escape! A bloody spy!

ROSALEEN *puts on the radio. A piece of Mozart plays.*

Rosaleen (*before the photograph*) Forgive me, Father. I've broken my claws and the jungle grows thicker by the minute. I tried . . . I tried, but I can't feel any vengeance –

Someone tries to open the door.

(*Shouting.*) Yes, I loved beside the Citadel that gave us five-eighths of a life!

Another heavy knock.

Wait! Be still. The teagues and the prods are clouds of scaldin' steam. (*Turning from the photo.*) My love, oh my love, my love, my love –

Man's Voice (*outside*) Open up in the name of the Central Council!

Rosaleen (*in a moment of terror*) Daddy! (*Turning away from the photograph.*) My love, my love, my love, oh my love –

Sadie's Voice Open up, you traitor-bitch, or we'll break the door down!

Rosaleen Its lonely in the distillation season.

She stands silent and unafraid as an axe splinters the wood of the door.

My love.

END OF PLAY